OPTIMAL ESTIMATION, IDENTIFICATION, AND CONTROL

ROBERT C. K. LEE

RESEARCH MONOGRAPH NO. 28
THE M.I.T. PRESS, CAMBRIDGE, MASSACHUSETTS

A PRAYER OF THANKSGIVING

Before God, all men are equally foolish, for we cannot begin to comprehend all the infinite mysteries surrounding us. If there be a grain of wisdom in this work, may it be to His glory, for He alone hath provided me with this splendid opportunity for learning, the wonderful parents, teachers and friends, a harmonious home, excellent health — and most of all, for the strength ever-sufficient from day to day.

Robert C. K. Lee

Third Printing, April 1970

ISBN 0 262 12012 7

Library of Congress Catalog Card Number: 64-25212

Printed in the United States of America

FOREWORD

There has long been a need in science and engineering for systematic publication of research studies larger in scope than a journal article but less ambitious than a finished book. Much valuable work of this kind is now published only in a semiprivate way, perhaps as a laboratory report, and so may not find its proper place in the literature of the field. The present contribution is the twenty-eighth of the M. I. T. Press Research Monographs, which we hope will make selected timely and important research studies readily accessible to libraries and to the independent worker.

J. A. Stratton

BASIC TERMINOLOGY AND DEFINITIONS

1. Unless otherwise specified, all upper case Roman or Greek letters represent matrices.
2. All lower case Roman or Greek letters represent (column) vectors. (Scalars will be specified.)
3. The transpose of a vector or matrix is denoted by a prime.
4. The norm and generalized norm are defined as $||x||^2 = x'x$ $||x||_R^2 = x'Rx$ respectively, where R is a weighting matrix.
5. The trace of a matrix A is defined as $\sum_{i=1}^{n} a_{ii}$
6. The gradient of J (a scalar) with respect to u is denoted by $\nabla_u J = \frac{\partial J}{\partial u}$. It is a row vector.
7. All rules of vector differentiation are according to that given in Appendix A.
8. The symbol $\triangleq$ implies a definition.
9. The symbol $\langle x, y \rangle$ denotes the scalar product of x and y $\equiv$ $x'y = y'x$ or $(x \cdot y)$.
10. The symbol $P(x|Z_n) \triangleq P(x|z_n, z_{n-1}, \cdots, z_1)$.

PREFACE

In the recent decade, considerable interest has arisen in the subject of modern control theory. This body of theory is a direct outgrowth of the desire to place the theory of automatic control on a firmer mathematical foundation. Much of the work done in this area is derived from the theory of optimization, and the problems are usually formulated and solved in the time domain using the concepts of state and matrix theory. Numerous contributions have been made in this pursuit, unfortunately with considerable differences in notation, emphasis, and interpretation. As a result, the language and concepts of modern control theory are often beyond the comprehension of practicing control engineers.

This thesis has been written from an engineer's point of view in that it emphasizes the relationship between concepts and the evolution of ideas rather than mathematical rigor. The text describes the basic concepts of the various known techniques in optimal control and estimation theory so that their similarities and limitations become apparent. Some logical extensions of this body of knowledge are then developed and discussed. Whenever possible, the notation is kept consistent and the explanations simplified to highlight the fundamental concepts involved.

In every stage of this research, the author has benefited from many invaluable suggestions and stimulating discussions with many individuals. First of all, he wishes to express his sincere appreciation to Professors Y. T. Li and W. E. Vander Velde of M.I.T. and Professor Y. C. Ho of Harvard University for their helpful suggestions, criticism, and guidance. The author is especially indebted to Professor Y. C. Ho, a good friend and a wonderful teacher, for his patience in helping him over the threshold of modern control theory, without which this work would not have been possible. To Professors R. L. Halfman and M. T. Landahl, the author is very grateful for their help in reviewing this manuscript and for making numerous constructive criticisms.

The author wishes to express his heartfelt gratitude also to Mr. Wally Lundahl and Mr. George Swanlund of the Honeywell Aeronautical Division for their encouragement and support of this undertaking, to the many engineers at Honeywell for their constructive criticism and invaluable discussions, and to Mr. Luther Prince, the author's former supervisor in industry, for helping him in the initial launching of his quest for higher learning.

The author wishes to acknowledge the assistance he received from Mr. George King of Honeywell in the preparation of the computational program. Acknowledgement is also made to the M.I.T. Computation Center for its work done as problem M3001. Last, but not least, the author wishes to express his deepest gratitude to his wife Bettie for her continuous encouragement in this undertaking.

Minneapolis, Minn.
July, 1964

Robert C. K. Lee

CONTENTS

Chapter 1

INTRODUCTION

A rather universal human desire is to obtain maximum return from our investments. This desire especially pervades business and engineering, where efficiency is usually a prerequisite to success. The type of problem in which we try to maximize the yield from our investment or to utilize our capabilities most efficiently is generally classified as an optimization problem.

From our daily experience, optimization problems often appear paradoxical. On one hand, such a problem may be so complicated by interrelated factors that it can hardly be defined properly, much less solved. On the other hand, striving for optimal solutions seems to be an inherent human goal.

From an analytical viewpoint, a typical optimization problem is composed of the following parts:

1. Definition of the goal.
2. Knowledge of our current position with respect to the goal.
3. Knowledge of our environment, including all the factors (social, economic, moral, physical) influencing our position in the past, present, and future.
4. Determination of the best policy from the definition (1) and knowledge (2 and 3).

To solve an optimization problem mathematically, we must (1) adequately define the problem in physical terms, (2) translate this physical description into mathematical language, and (3) solve this mathematical problem analytically. The first two tasks are often very difficult, since most physical problems are rather complicated and usually require compromises and tradeoffs that are quite difficult to define precisely. Also, the physical process or plant is never ideal; hence, we could never obtain an exact mathematical model for it. Even though the problem is specified in mathematical terms, the solution is still not an easy task. However, once it is well defined it can be attacked analytically in a systematic and scientific manner.

In the past decade, considerable interest in the field of optimization has been generated among engineers and scientists, largely because of the advent of the digital computer and the challenge of aerospace technology. As a result, various techniques and concepts have been contributed in this area, most of which were developed in the time domain using the concept of state and matrix theory. This body of knowledge may be classified loosely as "modern control theory."

In this thesis, our objective is to study the fundamental problems in control from the modern control theory point of view. We shall define the fundamental problem in control into five basic classes.

1.1 Deterministic-Control Problems

Consider the following problem:

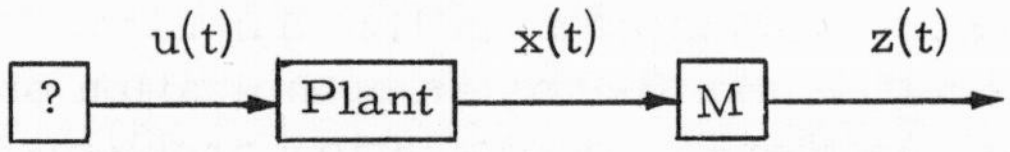

where M $\triangleq$ measurement device.

Given: The dynamic relationship between x and u, z and x.
Problem: Find the control u(t) such that the output x(t) or the measured output z(t) is more to "our liking."

Indeed this problem specification is extremely vague, since often the term "our liking" cannot be defined mathematically. For example, in flight-control work, it is well known that the pilot favors an aircraft with a short-period damping ratio of 0.7 and a natural frequency of 1/2 cps. No one can define exactly why this is so "mathematically" except that it just "feels" better. In many other control problems, "our liking" may imply a region in the x or z state space or a corridor in the x, t or z, t space (for example, trajectory problems), and the boundaries of these region or regions are not defined precisely. As a consequence of this ambiguity, quite often this control problem cannot be solved entirely in a mathematical manner, and the engineer has to rely on his "bag of tricks" for its solution. If the solution u(t) is a function of x(t) or z(t), we have the so-called "feedback" controller. In cases where the term "our liking" is a well-defined mathematical performance criterion, we can seek the best performance with respect to this criterion and have the optimal deterministic-control problem. In the latter case, the problem is well defined mathematically and, therefore, is amenable to analytical treatments.

1.2 Estimation Problem

This is the problem of estimating the states of the system in a stochastic environment. Consider the block diagram

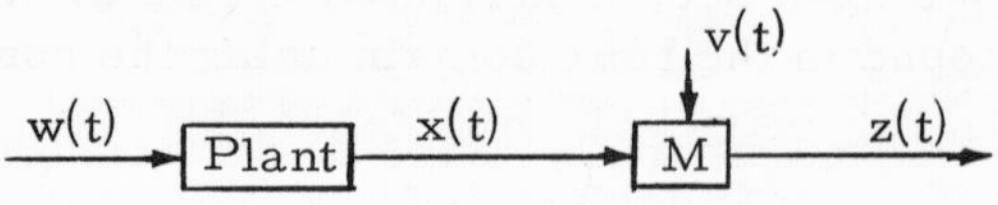

where M $\triangleq$ measurement device, w(t) is the driving noise vector and v(t) is the measurement noise vector.

Given: 1. The physical relationship between x and w.
2. The physical relationship between z and x, v.
3. The statistical description of w and v.

Problem: Given measurements z up to time T, find $\hat{x}(t/T)$ which is a best estimate of x_t in some sense. In the case where t = T, we have the "filtering" problem; where t > T, we have the prediction problem; where t < T, we have the smoothing problem. In general, this problem is well defined mathematically once the criterion for the "best" estimate is specified.

1.3 Stochastic-Control Problem

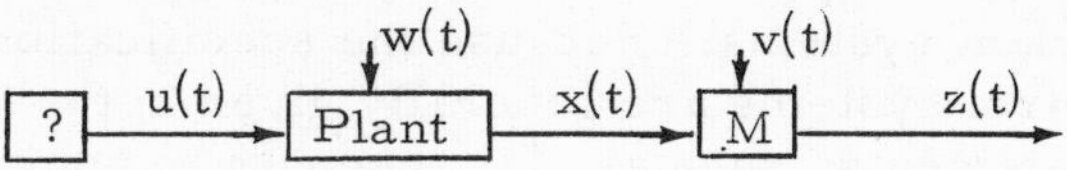

where M $\triangleq$ measurement device.

Given: 1. The physical relationship between x and w,u.
2. The physical relationship between z and x, v.
3. The statistical description of w, v.

Problem: Determine u(t) such that some estimate $\hat{x}$ of the state of the system is more to "our liking."

Analogous to the first problem, this is rather vague unless the term "our liking" is specified in terms of definite mathematical criteria. In the case where u(t) is to be determined as a function of z(t), we have the closed-loop stochastic-control problem.

1.4 Identification Problem

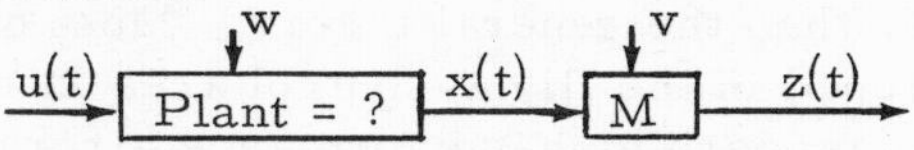

where M $\triangleq$ measurement device.

Given: 1. The statistical characteristics of w, v.
2. The physical relationship between z and x, v.
3. The measurable quantities are z and u.

Problem: Determine a best estimate of the plant (physical relationship between x and w, u) in some sense.

1.5 Adaptive-Control Problem

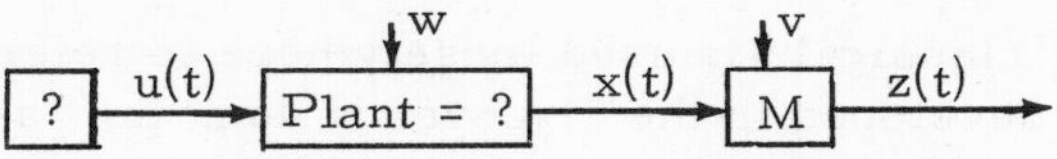

Given: 1. The statistical characteristics of w, v.
2. The physical relationship between z and x, v.
3. The measurable quantities are z, u.

Problem: Determine u(t) such that some estimate of the states x is more to "our liking." Analogous to problems 1.1 and 1.3, if u(t) is to be determined as a function of z(t), we have the closed-loop adaptive-control problem.

In classical control theory,† most of the work has been done in the frequency domain using the transform method. Considerable effort has been concentrated in the analysis of the first class of control problems; namely, the deterministic-control problem. Special emphasis is placed in the analysis of feedback control systems where stability and performance are of prime importance. Most design techniques were developed for the analysis of linear time-invariant systems. Because the specifications for the required control systems are generally given in the form of a list of word statements, such as, (1) response to command input, (2) response to disturbance input, (3) degree of stability, (4) allowable static and dynamic error, and so forth, the design procedure has been mostly trial and error with heavy reliance on various rules of thumb. Only recently has some emphasis been placed on the so-called analytical design techniques.[44] The basic idea is to put the specifications in the form of a more precise mathematical statement, that is, a performance index so that the overall system design is amenable to mathematical treatments. In the estimation area, the most notable work is that of the Wiener filter and its many modifications. In stochastic control, some techniques were developed using the analytical design procedure.[44] In the "identification" and "adaptive control" area, considerable work has been done in the past eight years.[15, 36, 37, 41-45, 55] These efforts have been concentrated in the development of specific systems rather than the general theory. Most of these techniques were developed in the flight-control area in response to the demand of the modern high-performance aircraft and missile requirement. Many of these systems were successfully flight tested.

In the domain of modern control theory, considerable knowledge has been obtained in the deterministic optimal-control area. Variou analytical techniques such as calculus of variations, dynamic programming, Pontryagin's maximum principles, and so forth, and computational techniques, such as, the gradient method, have been developed and are capable of treating time-varying, nonlinear control systems subjected to inequality constraints. In the estimation area, the most notable work is that due to Kalman,[26, 30, 31]

†The term "classical" is used loosely here to refer to a body of knowledge developed in the "frequency domain," using integral transform techniques.

namely, the Kalman filter or the Wiener-Kalman filter and its various modifications. In the stochastic-control area, little is known in general other than the separation theorem[9, 16, 20, 31, 54] developed for linear systems with Gaussian inputs. In the identification and adaptive control area, little general theory has been developed. Some effort[29, 34] has been spent in the extension of the Kalman filter to the identification problem with interesting computational results.[34]

The following chapters study the area of deterministic optimal control, estimation, identification, and their interrelations. Since these are very broad areas, an exhaustive coverage is not possible within the scope of this work. The basic aims of this study are (1) to survey the basic analytical and computational techniques in optimal control and estimation theory and present them in a coherent manner so that their similarities and differences as well as their relative merits will become apparent; (2) to provide some extensions and improvements when possible; (3) to formulate and solve the linear identification problem; and (4) to study the practical applications of these techniques in closed-loop systems.

Chapter 2

OPTIMAL-CONTROL THEORY

If we look into the recent literature in advanced control theory, we inevitably find that a large portion of the papers deal with the theoretical and practical aspects of optimal-control theory. Although many of these papers are poorly motivated and impractical from the engineering stand point, many of the techniques are very useful and are often necessary in many applications. One of the notable examples is the 50 percent reduction in time to climb over the best previously achieved results for a fighter aircraft. This was predicted by Bryson and verified by flight test. The advantages of optimal-control theory were also demonstrated in reducing aerodynamic heating in re-entry problems and other trajectory optimization problems. One of the major reasons attributable to the rise in popularity of optimal control is the advent of the modern high-speed digital computer. Without it the whole body of theory would be mostly abstract mathematics and would have very little engineering significance.

Most of the optimal-control techniques developed thus far are in the time domain using the concept of state and matrix theory. In general, the basic approach to the problem is as follows:

1. Define a cost function or index of performance (some precise mathematical measure of "goodness") of the system.
2. Determine the dynamic characteristics of the system in differential or difference equation form relating the state variables and control variables.
3. Specify certain equality or inequality constraints in the state variables or control variables, or both.

The objective is as follows: Given (2), optimize (1) subject to (3). The solution of this problem is often very complicated. Except for very simple cases, it cannot be done without the aid of a digital computer.

In this chapter, some of these basic concepts of optimal-control theory and their interrelations are discussed. The chief aim is to clarify the basic ideas rather than provide detailed instructions or rigorous derivations, since they can be found readily in the referenced literature. The discussion of optimal-control theory is divided into two basic sections: 2.1, the analytical methods and 2.2, the computational methods. The first section deals principally with the necessary conditions for optimality.

It consists of a discussion of the various approaches such as calculus of variation, dynamic programming, Pontryagin's maximum principle, and so forth, and their interrelations. The second section deals with the practical aspects of obtaining the numerical solution to the problem.

2.1 Analytical Methods

In this section, various techniques for determining the necessary condition for optimality are presented. These techniques are classified as analytical or indirect methods. As the name implies, these approaches do not seek the extremal solutions directly by comparisons or evaluations but rather seek to derive a set of conditions that the extremal solution must necessarily satisfy. For example, to find the minimum point of a single variable function $J = f(x)$, we may evaluate the function directly point by point for every x or indirectly by observing the fact that the minimum point must necessarily have zero slope, $df/dx = 0$. The chief advantage of the analytical methods is that once a solution is obtained, we have solved a whole class of problems rather than a specific one. It is this property that makes the analytical methods of great theoretical importance.

2.1.1 Ordinary Calculus Problem. We shall begin by studying the ordinary calculus problem of finding the stationary points of algebraic functions. Consider first the following case:

Single-stage process without constraints.

Problem: Consider a scalar function $J = J(x, u)$ without any constraints, where x is an n-vector, u is an m-vector, find x, u such that J is a minimum.

Solution: Necessary condition for stationarity

$$dJ = \frac{\partial J}{\partial u} du + \frac{\partial J}{\partial x} dx = \nabla_u J \, du + \nabla_x J \, dx = 0$$

Since the dx, du are arbitrary, the gradient $\nabla_u J$, $\nabla_x J$ must be zero at the stationary point. Sufficient condition: To find the sufficiency condition, consider a simple Taylor's series expansion about the stationary point.

$$\delta J = \frac{\partial J}{\partial u} du + \frac{\partial J}{\partial x} dx + [dx', du'] \begin{bmatrix} \frac{\partial^2 J}{\partial x^2} & \frac{\partial^2 J}{\partial x \, \partial u} \\ \frac{\partial^2 J}{\partial x \, \partial u} & \frac{\partial^2 J}{\partial u^2} \end{bmatrix} \begin{bmatrix} dx \\ du \end{bmatrix} + \cdots$$

$$= 0 + 0 + [dx', du'] \begin{bmatrix} D \end{bmatrix} \begin{bmatrix} dx \\ du \end{bmatrix} + \cdots$$

If the stationary point is a minimum, then δJ must be positive, hence [D] must be positive definite. This is often referred to as the Legendre-Clebsch condition.

Single-stage decision process with constraints.

Problem: Now we shall consider the problem of minimizing a function $J = J(x, u)$ subject to the vector constraints $f(x, u) = 0$. Unlike the previous case where we can look over the entire x, u space for the solution, we are now restricted to the subspace that satisfies the constraints $f(x, u) = 0$. In other words, the necessary condition for stationarity must be given by

$$\nabla_x J \Big|_{f(x,u)=0} = 0 \qquad \nabla_u J \Big|_{f(x,u)=0} = 0$$

Solution: To solve this problem, we introduce the method of Lagrange multipliers. Define a new function

$$J* = J + \langle \lambda \cdot f \rangle$$

where λ is a vector of the same dimension as f and is generally called the Lagrange multiplier vector. The necessary condition for stationarity is given by

$$\nabla_x J* = 0$$

$$\nabla_u J* = 0$$

$$\nabla_\lambda J* = 0$$

Note that we have the same number of equations as unknowns, hence the problem can be readily solved. Similar to the former case, the sufficient condition for a minimum will be that

$$D = \begin{bmatrix} \dfrac{\partial^2 J*}{\partial x^2} & \dfrac{\partial^2 J*}{\partial u\, \partial x} \\ \dfrac{\partial^2 J*}{\partial x\, \partial u} & \dfrac{\partial^2 J}{\partial u^2} \end{bmatrix}$$

is positive definite. It is interesting to note at this point that in all optimization problems, we always seek information about the gradient. In the case with no constraints, it is necessary that the gradient be zero at the stationary point. When subjected to constraints, the gradient need not be zero; however, it must be a linear combination of the gradients of the constrained equations. The coefficients of this linear combination are precisely the Lagrange multipliers. This fact can be interpreted geometrically as follows: The objective of the game is to make the first variation of J zero while satisfying the constraints. Therefore at the optimal point, the gradient vector must be orthogonal to the space of allowable x, u so that no further improvement is possible with perturbations in x, u. The space of allowable x, u consists of the intersections of the constraint surfaces in the state space; all the vectors in this space are simultaneously orthogonal to all the gradients of the constraint functions. Hence the gradient J must be given by a linear combination of all the gradients of the constraint functions. Knowing this relationship, we then look for what this linear combination must be; this is precisely the part played by the Lagrange multipliers. To further illustrate this idea, let us consider a simple three-dimensional example:

$$\text{Minimize } J = x_1^2 + x_2^2 + x_3^2$$

where J = constant, maps a sphere, subject to the constraints

$$f_1(x) = a'x + 1 = 0$$

$$f_2(x) = b'x + 1 = 0$$

For the sake of simplicity, let a' = (1, 0, 0) and b' = (0, 1, 0). Hence, the constraint surfaces are two planes and their intersection is as shown in Figure 2.1.

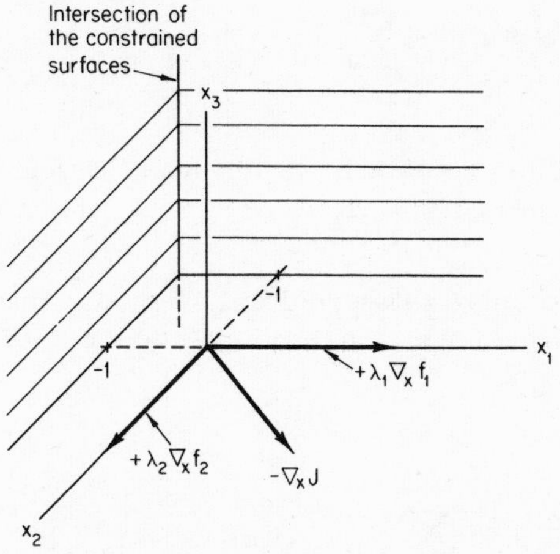

Figure 2.1. Geometric interpretation of the problem.

Inspecting the geometry of Figure 2.1, we can draw three immediate conclusions: (1) If the solution is to satisfy the constraints, it must lie on the line of intersections and this line must be perpendicular to the two gradients $\nabla_x f_1$, $\nabla_x f_2$. (2) The solution must be at a point where the line of intersection is tangent to the sphere J = constant. In other words, the gradient $\nabla_x J$ must also be perpendicular to the line of intersection. (3) Since $\nabla_x J$ must be perpendicular to the line of intersection, it must lie in a plane spanned by the gradients of the two constraint surfaces $\nabla_x f_1$, $\nabla_x f_2$ (see Figure 1), hence, it can be expressed as linear combination of $\nabla_x f_1$ and $\nabla_x f_2$. The coefficients of this linear combination are precisely the Lagrange multipliers. Consequently, we can conclude by inspection that the solution must be $x = \begin{bmatrix} -1 \\ -1 \\ 0 \end{bmatrix}$ and $\nabla_x J = [-2, -2, 0]$. Thus, the Lagrange multiplier must be +2, +2. This solution can be readily verified by direct computation.

Multistage decision processes with constraints. Now we shall extend the concept of the previous section to the solution of a multistage problem. Here the constraint equation is given in the form of a difference equation,

$$x_{i+1} = f(x_i, u_i, i)$$

where x_0 is given and $i = 0, 1, \cdots, n - 1$; and the performance criterion is

$$J = \phi[x(n)] + \sum_{i=0}^{n-1} L_i(x_i, u_i)$$

Problem: The problem is as follows: Given x_0, find the sequence u_i, where $i = 0, 1, 2, \cdots n - 1$, that minimize (maximizes) J.

Solution: To solve this problem, we again introduce the Lagrange multipliers, which are now a sequence of vectors. Hence, define

$$J^* \triangleq J + \sum_{i=0}^{n-1} \lambda_{i+1}' [f(x_i, u_i) - x_{i+1}]$$

This is a multivector variable optimization problem with the necessary conditions being given by a set of 3(n) equations.

$$\nabla_{u_0} J^* = 0 = \frac{\partial L_0}{\partial u_0} + \lambda_1' \frac{\partial f_0}{\partial u_0}$$

$$\begin{cases} \nabla_{x_1} J^* = 0 = \dfrac{\partial L_1}{\partial x_1} + \lambda_2' \dfrac{\partial f_1}{\partial x_1} - \lambda_1' \\ \nabla_{u_1} J^* = 0 = \dfrac{\partial L_1}{\partial u_1} + \lambda_2' \dfrac{\partial f_1}{\partial u_1} \\ \nabla_{\lambda_1} J^* = 0 = [f_0(x_0, u_0, 0) - x_1]' \end{cases}$$

$$\vdots$$

$$\begin{cases} \nabla_{x_{n-1}} J^* = 0 = \dfrac{\partial L_{n-1}}{\partial x_{n-1}} + \lambda_n' \dfrac{\partial f_{n-1}}{\partial x_{n-1}} - \lambda_{n-1}' \\ \nabla_{u_{n-1}} J^* = 0 = \dfrac{\partial L_{n-1}}{\partial u_{n-1}} + \lambda_n' \dfrac{\partial f_{n-1}}{\partial u_{n-1}} \\ \nabla_{\lambda_{n-1}} J^* = 0 = [f_{n-2}(x_{n-2}, u_{n-2}) - x_{n-1}]' \end{cases}$$

$$\begin{cases} \nabla_{x_n} J^* = 0 = \dfrac{\partial \phi[x(n)]}{\partial x_n} - \lambda_n' \\ \nabla_{\lambda_n} J^* = 0 = [f_{n-1}(x_{n-1}, u_{n-1}) - x_n]' \end{cases}$$

Putting them into compact difference equation form, we have

$$\lambda_i' = \frac{\partial L_i}{\partial x_i} + \lambda_{i+1}' \frac{\partial f_i}{\partial x_i} \qquad \lambda_n' = \frac{\partial \phi(x_n)}{\partial x_n}$$

$$x_i = f_{i-1}(x_{i-1}, u_{i-1}) \qquad x_0 \text{ given}$$

$$\frac{\partial \mathcal{H}_i}{\partial u_i} = 0$$

Where, $\mathcal{H}_i \stackrel{\Delta}{=} L_i + \lambda_{i+1}' f_i$ (often called the "Hamiltonian"). (Note that we can conclude immediately from these equations that the Hamiltonian must be stationary with respect to u along the optimal trajectory.) The boundary condition is given by x_0 and

$\lambda_n = \left[\frac{\partial\phi(x_n)}{\partial x_n}\right]'$. This is an example of a so-called two-point boundary-value problem with split boundary conditions. Such problems are usually very difficult to solve even with the modern high-speed computer. The computational problem will be discussed in more detail in the sequel (see Section 2.2.1). Hereafter, the phrase "two-point boundary-value problem" will be abbreviated as "TPBVP."

2.1.2 The Calculus of Variation Problem. In this section, the problem of finding the extremum of a continuous process is discussed. Let us begin by treating the classical problem of Bolza.

Problem: Given a continuous dynamic process described by the differential equation

$$\dot{x} = f(x, u, t) \qquad x_0 \text{ given} \tag{2.1}$$

find u so as to minimize

$$J = \phi[x(T)] + \int_{t_0}^{T} L(x, u, t)\, dt \tag{2.2}$$

Solution: Introduce a Lagrange multiplier vector function $\lambda(t)$, then the problem becomes

$$\text{Minimize } J^* \triangleq \phi[x(T)] + \int_{t_0}^{T} L(x, u, t)\, dt$$

$$- \int_{t_0}^{T} \langle\lambda(t) \cdot [\dot{x} - f(x, u, t)]\rangle\, dt$$

$$= \phi\,[x(T)] + \int_{t_0}^{T} F(x, u, \lambda, t)\, dt \tag{2.3}$$

subject to no constraints. It follows immediately from classical variational calculus that the Euler-Lagrange equations are

$$\left.\begin{aligned} \frac{\partial F}{\partial x} - \frac{d}{dt}\frac{\partial F}{\partial \dot{x}} &= 0 \\ \frac{\partial F}{\partial u} - \frac{d}{dt}\frac{\partial F}{\partial \dot{u}} &= 0 \\ \frac{\partial F}{\partial \lambda} - \frac{d}{dt}\frac{\partial F}{\partial \dot{\lambda}} &= 0 \end{aligned}\right\} \tag{2.4}$$

Now, let us define a function called the Hamiltonian

$$\mathcal{H}(x, u, \lambda, t) \triangleq \langle \lambda \cdot f(x, u, t) \rangle + L(x, u, t) \tag{2.5}$$

then we have

$$F = -\lambda'\dot{x} + \mathcal{H}(x, u, \lambda, t) \tag{2.6}$$

therefore,

$$\frac{\partial F}{\partial \dot{x}} = -\lambda' \qquad \frac{\partial F}{\partial x} = \frac{\partial \mathcal{H}}{\partial x} \qquad \frac{\partial F}{\partial u} = \frac{\partial \mathcal{H}}{\partial u}$$

$$\frac{\partial F}{\partial \dot{u}} = 0 = \frac{\partial F}{\partial \dot{\lambda}} \qquad \frac{\partial F}{\partial \lambda} = -[\dot{x} - f(x, u, t)]'$$

Substituting into Equations 2.4, we have the necessary condition

$$\left.\begin{aligned} \frac{d}{dt}\lambda &= -\left[\frac{\partial \mathcal{H}(x, u, \lambda, t)}{\partial x}\right]' \\ \frac{dx}{dt} &= f(x, u, t) \\ \frac{\partial \mathcal{H}}{\partial u} &= 0 \end{aligned}\right\} \tag{2.7}$$

The boundary conditions are x_0 and $\lambda_T = \dfrac{\partial \phi[x(T)]'}{\partial x(T)}$. Here, once again, we have the necessary condition for optimality characterized by a two-point boundary-value problem. The only difference here is that we have differential equations instead of the difference equations given in the last section. Note also that the Hamiltonian $\mathcal{H}$ must be stationary with respect to u along the optimal trajectory. The earlier derivation assumes continuity and various smoothness conditions; if these are not satisfied, the Euler-Lagrange equations do not exist. Furthermore, we have not taken into consideration any constraints on u. Hence, for problems where the loss function L does not contain u, impractical solutions may result. (That is, $u = \pm\infty$.) Equation 2.7 can be written also in the following form

$$\left.\begin{aligned} \dot{\lambda} &= -\left[\frac{\partial \mathcal{H}^0}{\partial x}\right]' \\ \dot{x} &= \left[\frac{\partial \mathcal{H}^0}{\partial \lambda}\right]' \end{aligned}\right\} \tag{2.8}$$

where $\mathcal{H}^0(x, \lambda, t) \triangleq \mathcal{H}(x, u^0, \lambda, t)$ and u^0 satisfied the equation $(\partial\mathcal{H}/\partial u) = 0$. These are often referred to as the canonical equations of Hamilton.

2.1.3 Application of the Caratheodory Lemma. This approach starts with the Caratheodory lemma[28] which states that if there exists a function $k(x, t)$ in a region of the state space G, such that

1. $\dfrac{\partial k(x,t)}{\partial t}$, $\dfrac{\partial k(x,t)}{\partial x}$ exists
2. $k(x, t) \in U(t)$ — an allowable set
3. $L^*(x, k, t) = 0$
4. $L^*(x, u, t) > 0$ for all $u \neq k(x, t)$

Let ϕ^0 be the solution to $\dot{x} = f(x, k, t)$, where $x(t_0) = x_0$, and remain entirely in G. Also let $\phi(x, T) = 0$ if x belongs to the target set S. Then, (a)

$$J^* = \int_{t_0}^{T} L^*(x, k, t)\, dt = 0 \text{ (unique absolute min)}$$

and (b) ϕ^0 is the optimal motion, hence $k(x, t)$ is the optimal contr To put it in another way, we can say that the Caratheodory lemma states a sufficient condition which characterizes an optimal control. To apply the Caratheodory lemma to our problem of minimizing

$$J(x_0, t_0) = \phi(x_T, T) + \int_{t_0}^{T} L(x, u, t)\, dt$$

subjected to the constraints $\dot{x} = f(x, u, t)$ where t_0, x_0 are given, we need a few transformations. The objective is to change our problem into the form of the lemma, so that the results apply. We proceed as follows:

1. Assume that the yet unknown optimal criterion function $J^0(x, t)$ exists and is twice differentiable in x and t such that

$$\int_{t_0}^{T} \left[\frac{dJ^0(x,t)}{dt}\right] dt = \int_{t_0}^{T} \left[< \frac{\partial J^0(x,t)}{\partial x}, \dot{x} > + \frac{\partial J^0(x,t)}{\partial t}\right] dt$$

$$\equiv J^0(x_T, T) - J^0(x_0, t_0)$$

2. Adding and subtracting this equation from our criterion, we have

$$J(x_0, t_0) = \phi(x_T, T) + \int_{t_0}^{T} \left[L(x,u,t) + <\dot{x}, \frac{\partial J^0(x,t)}{\partial x}> + \frac{\partial J^0}{\partial t}\right] dt$$

$$- J^0(x_T, T) + J^0(x_0, t_0)$$

$$= \phi(x_T, T) - J^0(x_T, T)$$

$$+ \int_{t_0}^{T} \left[H + \frac{\partial J^0(x,t)}{\partial t}\right] dt + J^0(x_0, t_0)$$

where

$$H \triangleq H\left(x, \frac{\partial J^0}{\partial x}, u, t\right) \triangleq L(x,u,t) + <\dot{x}, \frac{\partial J^0}{\partial x}>$$

3. Let $u^0(x, \partial J^0/\partial x, t)$ be the unknown optimal control function that minimizes the H function.

$$H^0\left(x, \frac{\partial J^0}{\partial x}, t\right) \triangleq \min_u H\left(x, \frac{\partial J^0}{\partial x}, u, t\right)$$

$$= H\left(x, u^0, \frac{\partial J^0}{\partial x}, t\right)$$

where

$$u^0 \triangleq u\left(x, \frac{\partial J^0}{\partial x}, t\right)$$

4. Now since $J^0(x,t)$ is the optimal criterion function by definition, then assuming that it is unique, we must have

$$J^0(x_T, T) = \phi(x_T, T)$$

Hence from statement 2, we have

$$J(x_0, t_0) - J^0(x_0, t_0) = \int_{t_0}^{T} \left[H + \frac{\partial J^0(x,t)}{\partial t} \right] dt \geq 0$$

Using the optimal control u^0, we have

$$J(x_0, t_0) - J^0(x_0, t_0) \equiv 0 = \int_{t_0}^{T} \left[H^0 + \frac{\partial J^0(x,t)}{\partial t} \right] dt$$

$$= \int_{t_0}^{T} L* \, dt = J*$$

5. In other words, if $J^0(x, t)$ is the optimal criterion function, then it must satisfy the partial differential equations

$$\frac{\partial J^0(x,t)}{\partial t} + H^0 \left(x, \frac{\partial J^0(x,t)}{\partial x}, t \right) = 0$$

with the boundary condition $J^0(x_T, T) = \phi(x_T, T)$.

This is often referred to as the Hamilton-Jacobi partial differential equation (H-JPDE). It is both necessary and sufficient. It is, in general, very difficult to solve; however, once it is solved, we will have a closed-loop control law in that $u = u^0(x, t)$. So far there exist only a few cases, such as the linear system with quadratic criterion, and so forth, for which the H-JPDE has been successfully solved. Because of the difficulties in solving partial differential equations, one can convert the H-JPDE into two sets of canonical equations as follows: Define

$$\left. \frac{\partial J^0(x,t)'}{\partial x} \right|_{\text{a.o.t.}} \triangleq p(x_0, t_0, t) = p(t)$$

where a.o.t. abbreviates "along an optimal trajectory."

$$\frac{d}{dt} p(t) = \frac{d}{dt} \left(\left. \frac{\partial J^0}{\partial x} \right|_{\text{a.o.t.}} \right) = \left[\left. \frac{\partial}{\partial t} \frac{\partial J^0}{\partial x} \right|_{\text{a.o.t.}} + \left. \frac{\partial^2 J'}{\partial x^2} \right|_{\text{a.o.t.}} \dot{x} \right]$$

Differentiation of H-JPDE by parts with respect to x along the optimal trajectory gives

$$-\frac{\partial^2 J^0(x,t)}{\partial x\,\partial t} = \frac{\partial L}{\partial x} + \left[\frac{\partial^2 J^0(x,t)'}{\partial x^2}\dot{x}\right] + \frac{\partial J^0(x,t)}{\partial x}\frac{\partial f'(x,u^0,t)}{\partial x} + \frac{\partial H^0}{\partial u^0}\frac{\partial u^0}{\partial x}$$

where $\partial H^0/\partial u^0 = 0$. Substituting into the previous equation, we have

$$\frac{d}{dt}p(t) = -\frac{\partial L(x,u^0,t)'}{\partial x} - \frac{\partial f(x,u^0,t)'}{\partial x}p$$

This is the Euler-Lagrange equation in the calculus of variations. Now we will define the Hamiltonian $\mathcal{H} \triangleq L(x,u,t) + \langle\dot{x},p\rangle$. Then $\mathcal{H}^0 \triangleq \min_u \mathcal{H} = p' f(x,u^0,t) + L(x,u^0,t) = \mathcal{H}^0(x,p,t)$, therefore, $u^0 = u(x,p,t)$ and we have

$$\frac{d}{dt}p(t) = -\left[\frac{\partial \mathcal{H}^0(x,p,t)}{\partial x}\right]' \qquad p(T) = \left[\frac{\partial J^0}{\partial x}\bigg|_T\right]'$$

Also along the optimal trajectory, we must have

$$\frac{d}{dt}x = f(x,u^0,t) = \left[\frac{\partial \mathcal{H}^0(x,p,t)}{\partial p}\right] \qquad x(t_0) = x_0$$

These are so-called canonical equations of Hamilton. Here, we have again the conditions for optimality characterized by a two-point boundary-value problem identical to that derived previously. Also, p is often called the costate vector. Note that for cases where there is no constraint in u, then p(t) will be identical to the Lagrange multiplier vector $\lambda(t)$ in the calculus of variation problem.

2.1.4 Dynamic Programming.† In this section, we derive the necessary conditions using the dynamic programming approach. The basic concept of dynamic programming will be discussed later in Section 2.2.2.

Problem: We proceed by considering the basic problem of minimizing

$$J = \phi[x(T),T] + \int_{t_0}^{T} L(x,u,t)\,dt$$

Subject to the constraints $\dot{x} = f(x,u,t)$ and x_0 given.

Solution: Define a function $J^0(x,t) \triangleq$ optimal value of J starting at x and t and using optimal control. Then from the principle of optimality, we must have

†See References 4, 5, 9, and 20 for additional details.

$$J^0(x,t) = \min_u [L\ \Delta t + J^0(x + \Delta x,\ t + \Delta t)]$$

$$\leq L\ \Delta t + J^0(x + \Delta x, t + \Delta t)$$

Assuming that the Taylor's series expansion of $J^0(x,t)$ exists, (this is a fundamental assumption), then we have

$$J^0(x,t) = \min_u \left[L\ \Delta t + J^0(x,t) + \frac{\partial J^0}{\partial t}\ \Delta t + \left(\frac{\partial J^0}{\partial x}\right)\ \Delta x + \text{higher order terms} \right]$$

Cancelling $J^0(x,t)$ from both sides and dividing by Δt and passing to the limit as $\Delta t \to 0$, we have

$$0 = \min_u \left[L(x,u,t) + \frac{\partial J^0(x,t)}{\partial t} + \frac{\partial J^0(x,t)}{\partial x}\,\dot{x} \right]$$

or

$$-\frac{\partial J^0(x,t)}{\partial t} = \min_u \left[L(x,u,t) + \frac{\partial J^0(x,t)}{\partial x}\,\dot{x} \right]$$

This is often referred to as Bellman's equation. It is both necessary and sufficient. Now if the bracketed quantity is continuous in the u space, and u is not constrained, then $\partial[\ ]/\partial u$ exists. Setting $\partial[\ ]/\partial u = 0$ (necessary condition), we obtain the relationship $u^0 = u(x, \partial J^0/\partial x, t)$. Substituting u^0 into the Bellman equation, we have

$$-\frac{\partial J^0}{\partial t} = L(x, u^0, t) + \frac{\partial J^0}{\partial x}\,\dot{x} \triangleq H^0\left(x, \frac{\partial J^0}{\partial x}, t\right)$$

This is the Hamilton-Jacobi partial differential equation. If $u^0 = u(x, \partial J^0/\partial x, t)$ indeed minimizes the $[L + (\partial J^0/\partial x)\,\dot{x}]$, then this equation is again both necessary and sufficient. Based on the original criterion function, the boundary condition for both the Bellman and the H-JPDE must be $J^0(x_T, T) = \phi(x_T, T)$. If the Bellman equation could be solved, we would have a closed-loop control law even for cases where u is constrained. Unfortunately, methods for the general solution of such an equation are not available.

Analogous to the previous case discussed in Section 2.1.3, the H-JPDE could be easily reduced to the canonical equations of Hamilton,

$$\dot{p} = -\left[\frac{\partial \mathcal{H}^0}{\partial x}\right]' \qquad p(T) = \frac{\partial J^0(x_T, T)}{\partial x_T}$$

$$\dot{x} = \left[\frac{\partial \mathcal{H}^0}{\partial p}\right]' \qquad x(t_0) = x_0$$

Where, $\mathcal{H}^0 \triangleq \mathcal{H}(x, u^0, p, t) = \mathcal{H}^0(x, p, t)$ (Hamiltonian), and $u^0 = u(x, p, t)$ (optimal control which satisfies) $\partial\mathcal{H}/\partial u = 0$, and

$$p(t) \triangleq \left[\frac{\partial J^0(x, t)}{\partial x}\right]'\Bigg|_{a.o.t.}$$

Here we convert the H-JPDE into 2n ordinary differential equations with split-end conditions that are slightly easier to handle.

2.1.5 The Maximum Principle of Pontryagin.† One of the more outstanding recent contributions to optimal control theory is the maximum principle of L.S. Pontryagin. This principle was discovered by Pontryagin and his colleagues in 1956. The essence of the maximum principle is that it enables us to handle variational problems with constraints of boundedness in the control variables where the classical calculus of variation no longer holds. In recent literature,[11] the maximum principle has been extended to the case where the state variables are subjected to inequality constraint also. In Chapter 2 of Reference 48, Pontryagin presented a detailed and elegant proof of the maximum principle. Since this proof is rather involved, it is not repeated here. In what follows, the maximum principle is presented in a slightly modified form from that originally presented by Pontryagin, although the proof and results remain the same. The modification introduced is necessary to make the terminology conform to that of the previous sections. For consistency, the following should perhaps be referred to as[2] the "minimum principle."‡

The minimum principle:

Problem: Given a performance criterion

$$J = \phi[x(T)] + \int_{t_0}^{T} L(x, u, t)\, dt$$

subject to the constraints

---

†See References 2, 11, 39, 48, and 52 for details.

‡The modification is that in a minimization problem, it is necessary that the Hamiltonian be minimized instead of maximized as originally presented in the maximum principle.

$$\dot{x} = f(x, u, t)$$

$$x_0 \text{ given}$$

$$u(t) \in \Omega \text{ (some subset in the u space)}$$

find u(t) such that J is minimized.

Solution:

1. Form the Hamiltonian

$$\mathcal{H}(x, p, u, t) \triangleq \langle \dot{x}, p(t) \rangle + L(x, u, t)$$

where p(t) is the costate vector and is a function of time only.

2. Find the control $u^0(x, p, t)$ which minimizes $\mathcal{H}$, that is,

$$\mathcal{H}^0(x, p, t) \triangleq \min_{u \in \Omega} \mathcal{H}(x, p, u, t)$$

3. Solve the set of canonical equations:

$$\dot{x} = \left[\frac{\partial \mathcal{H}^0}{\partial p}\right]' \qquad x(t_0) = x_0$$

$$\dot{p} = -\left[\frac{\partial \mathcal{H}^0}{\partial x}\right]'$$

p(T) are specified according to the constraints on x(T), for example, for free end conditions (x_T not specified)

$$p(T) = \left[\frac{\partial \phi[x(T)]}{\partial x_T}\right]'$$

For details on other end conditions see References 39, 48, and 52.

Here we encounter once again the two-point boundary-value problems of the previous section. The only difference is that the control vector u could be constrained. Hence $\partial \mathcal{H}/\partial u$ need not exist everywhere.

Theorem 2.1.† If $u^0(t)$ is the optimal control in that it minimizes the performance criterion J, then it satisfies the minimum condition of the Hamiltonian $\mathcal{H}$. (In other words, minimizing $\mathcal{H}$ is a necessary condition for optimal control. In many problems, we can show uniqueness of $u^0(t)$, hence this condition is also sufficient.)

Theorem 2.2.† For systems of the type

†Slightly modified from that of Reference 52.

$$\dot{x} = A(t)x + B(t)u$$

and free right end conditions, the necessary and sufficient condition for optimal control u(t) is the fulfillment of the minimum condition of the Hamiltonian $\mathcal{H}$.

At this point, we see that the minimum principle of Pontryagin affords us a neat way of confidently writing down the necessary conditions for the optimum even when u(t) is bounded. Further, the minimum condition of the Hamiltonian will provide the form of the optimal control u(t) as a function of x, p, t; this in turn enables one to set up the canonical equations. Although the minimum principle does not circumvent the computational difficulties of the two-point boundary-value problem, in some cases it does provide considerable insight into the form of the optimal control function so that we may be able to solve the problem indirectly.[2,48] For example, in any problem where the control enters linearly in the constrain equation $\dot{x} = f(x, u, t)$ and linearly or not at all in the loss function $L(x, u, t)$ (for example, time optimal-control problem) then from the minimum principle we obtain immediately that the control will be always on the boundary. For the time optimal-control case, this behavior is often referred to as the bang-bang control principle. It can be easily demonstrated as follows:
Let

$$J = \int_0^T dt \qquad L = 1$$

$$\dot{x} = Ax + bu \qquad u \text{ scalar}$$

$$|u| \leq 1\cdot 0$$

then following the minimum principle, we have

1. $\mathcal{H} = \langle \dot{x}, p \rangle + 1$

$$= 1 + x'A'p + ub'p$$

2. The minimum condition of the Hamiltonian states that $u = -(1) \operatorname{sign}(b'p)$. Hence we know that the control will be ± 1 and it switches when $b'p$ changes sign. This type of information often simplifies the solution of the TPBVP .

2.1.6 Summary. In this first half of Chapter 2, various analytical approaches to the optimization problem have been discussed. It was shown that all these methods converge to the same basic set of ordinary differential equations (a two-point boundary-value problem) as the necessary conditions for optimality. It was demonstrated that in all cases, the Hamiltonian must be stationary with respect to u along the optimal trajectory. In the case where the control vector u is not constrained, the Lagrange multiplier vector λ used in the calculus of variation is identical to the co-state vector defined in subsequent derivations. The objective has been to show that the same necessary conditions for optimality can be derived by various means, the only differences are the various restrictions involved in its derivation. In the case of calculus of variation and ordinary calculus, free variation must be allowed; in other words, all the derivatives involved must exist and be continuous and smooth throughout the interval. In the Caratheodory lemma, the optimal loss function J must also be smooth. In the dynamic programming approach, however, the basic restriction is the smoothness and continuous condition of the optimal return function J. This will insure the validity of the Taylor's series expansion of Section 2.1.4. With this assumption, we can readily obtain the Bellman equation.

$$-\frac{\partial J^0(x,t)}{\partial t} = \min_u \left[L(x,u,t) + \frac{\partial J^0(x,t)}{\partial x}\dot{x} \right] \qquad J^0(x_T, T) = \phi(x_T)$$

This is both necessary and sufficient. If the bracketed quantity is continuous and smooth in the u space so that $\partial[\,]/\partial u$ exists, we obtain the Hamilton-Jacobi partial differential equation,

$$-\frac{\partial J^0(x,t)}{\partial t} = \mathcal{H}^0\left(x, \frac{\partial J^0}{\partial x}, t\right)$$

From this equation, it was shown in Section 2.1.3 that the canonica equations can be readily derived. In formulating his maximum principle, Pontryagin showed that the canonical equations are valid without the smoothness restriction in both the optimal return function J and the control vector u. (This is the major contribution of the maximum principle.) In addition Pontryagin provides a systematic procedure for handling the optimization probler with bounded control variables and offers some physical insight into the form of the optimal control function.

Finally, it must be emphasized again that our aim here is to discuss the basic concepts of various approaches and to point out their similarities and differences. The restrictions discussed earlier on the various methods are inherent but not necessarily absolute. With ingenuity, these restrictions can be and have been overcome in many cases. Indeed, volumes of literature have been written on various extensions and modifications of the calculus of variations alone. To cover all the details on each method will only obscure our fundamental aim; hence, they will not be included.

2.2 Computational Methods

In the previous sections, various necessary conditions for optimality were presented and discussed. It was shown that the necessary conditions are a set of two-point boundary-value problems. This type of solution may be very elegant and satisfying to the mathematician; they are of little value to the engineer unless numerical solutions could be readily obtained. In what follows, three basic numerical techniques are presented. Their difficulties and merits are discussed. The first method deals with the direct solution of the two-point boundary-value problem. The method of dynamic programming and gradients, presented subsequently, are for direct solutions of extremal problems.

2.2.1 Computational Solutions of the Two-Point Boundary-Value Problem (Solutions in the Multiplier Space). One of the chief drawbacks of the analytical methods discussed previously is the difficulty of obtaining solutions for the two-point boundary-value problem. Only in very rare cases (that is, linear system, quadratic criterion, no constraints) can a closed-form solution be found. In general, we must try to obtain numerical solutions with the aid of computers. Unfortunately, even with the advent of the modern high-speed digital computer, the solution of the TPBVP is still at best a very difficult task. The reasons for this difficulty are best illustrated by considering the following example:

Given: A set of differential equations obtained in a minimum "terminal norm" problem,

$$\dot{x} = f(x, u^0, t) \qquad x_0, p_T \text{ given}$$

$$\dot{p} = -A'p$$

$$u^0 = u(x, p, t)$$

where

$$A \triangleq \frac{\partial f}{\partial x}$$

evaluated along the optimal trajectory.

Problem: Find the optimal trajectory and control solution described by these equations.

The difficulties in obtaining such a solution are

1. Two-point split-boundary condition: The modern analogue and digital computers are highly efficient in solving high-order initial-value problems. In other words, we can program the differential (difference) equations in the computer; then, given the

initial values, the computer can perform integrations with both speed and precision. With boundary conditions specified at both ends (some initial and some final), the problem is not quite as simple. To solve the problem, we must first obtain a complete set of initial conditions namely, x_0 and p_0. Since p_0 is not given, we must guess one. Once p_0, x_0 are obtained, we can determine u_0^0, A_0 and the equations can be integrated forward one step. At the end of the step x_1, p_1 are used to determine u_1^0, A_1 and the process is repeated up to the final time T. At time T, the solution p_T obtained is compared with that originally given. If they do not agree, a new p_0 is guessed and the procedure repeated until the results are "close enough." This trial-and-error process is extremely laborious and often impractical for high-order nonlinear systems.

2. Instability of the costate equation: In most TPBVP arising from the analytical methods discussed in the previous sections, the costate equations (often called the Euler-Lagrange equation, the multiplier equation, and sometimes mistakenly referred to as the adjoint equation†) are often unstable when integrating forward, ($-A'$ has positive eigenvalues). This means that a small error in guessing the initial values will cause a very large error at the end, making it even more difficult to make the computational process converge to the correct solution.

3. Constraints: The presence of constraints on the optimization problem, for example, $|u| \leq 1$, causes additional difficulties. As pointed out in the previous sections, the presence of constraints implies that a free variation about the extremal is not allowed when the boundary is reached. This theoretically invalidates the Euler equation. However, Pontryagin's maximum principle still holds (see Section 2.1.5), and we will still have a TPBVP that characterizes the extremal solution. The reason that constraints cause additional difficulties can be demonstrated by considering Figure 2.2. Here, not only must we guess the missing initial conditions

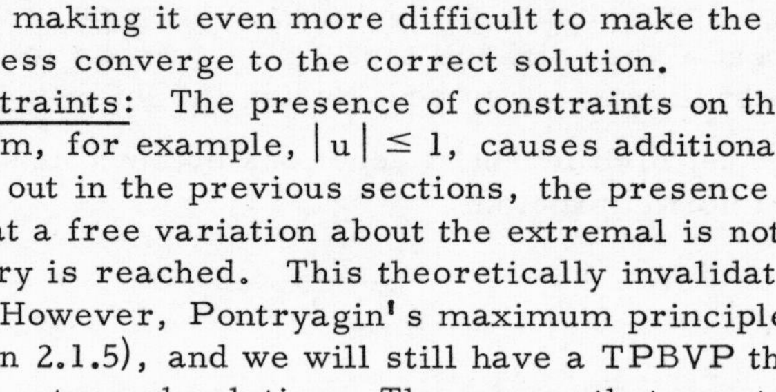

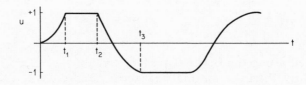

Figure 2.2. Constraints on the optimization problem.

†It becomes the adjoint equation only in the Mayer problem (in the Mayer problem $J = \phi[x(T)]$, $L = 0$) or in cases where L is not a function of the states (that is, time optimal control).

but the time for getting on and off the boundary must be guessed as well. In other words, the error in the terminal condition is sensitive not only to the error in guessing the initial conditions but also to the time the control gets on and off the boundary.

As a consequence of these difficulties, this method of computation is often impractical for most applications. Some notable exceptions are the problems associated with nondissipative systems, that is, mid-course guidance, and so forth, where the system and its costate are both neutrally stable.

2.2.2 Dynamic Programming. Another technique for obtaining numerical solutions is via the method of dynamic programming. This approach was first introduced by R. Bellman.[4, 5] Basically, this is a functional equation approach to the determination of extremums of Markovian-type processes. Before we can proceed further, two basic concepts should be defined.

1. Markovian-type processes: A function $f(p_1, p_2, \cdots, p_n, g_1, \cdots, g_n)$ is said to possess a Markovian nature if after a number of decisions, say k, the effect of the remaining n - k decisions upon the total return depends only upon the state of the system after the k-th decision and subsequent decisions.[5] (In general, a function whose variables can be related by ordinary differential or difference equations (linear or nonlinear) of finite-order can be considered "Markovian.")

2. Principle of optimality (Markovian processes): An optimal policy has the property that whatever the initial state and the initial decision are, the remaining decisions must constitute an optimal policy with regard to the state resulting from the first decision.[5]

Using these two basic concepts, one can convert an n-stage extremum process into n-single-stage decision processes that are related recursively. To illustrate this point, let us consider the problem of finding an extremal of

$$J = \int_0^T L(x, u)\, dt \cong \sum_{i=0}^{n-1} L(x_i, u_i)\,\Delta \qquad T = n\Delta$$

subject to the constraints

$$x_{i+1} = f(x_i, u_i, \Delta) \qquad x_0 \text{ given}$$

Here, we have an n-stage process, in which we seek the n control vectors $u_0, u_1, \cdots, u_{n-1}$ that will minimize $J(x_0)$. The dynamic programming approach sets up the functional relations as follows: Let $J_n(x_0)$ = optimal cost function for an n-stage process starting at x_0. Then we must have, from the principle of optimality,

$$J_n(x_0) = \min_{u_0} [L(x_0, u_0)\Delta + J_{n-1}(x_1)]$$

where

$$x_1 = f(x_0, u_0, \Delta)$$

Similarly by induction, we have

$$J_{n-1}(x_1) = \min_{u_1} [L(x_1, u_1)\Delta + J_{n-2}(x_2)]$$

$$x_2 = f(x_1, u_1, \Delta)$$

$$\vdots$$

$$J_2(x_{n-2}) = \min_{u_{n-2}} [L(x_{n-2}, u_{n-2})\Delta + J_1(x_{n-1})]$$

$$x_{n-1} = f(x_{n-2}, u_{n-2}, \Delta)$$

$$J_1(x_{n-1}) = \min_{u_{n-1}} [L(x_{n-1}, u_{n-1})\Delta]$$

Using this set of recursive relationships, we solve the problem backward starting with $J_1(x_{n-1})$. From $J_1(x_{n-1})$ we can compute $J_2(x_{n-2})$, and so on.

Computation procedure: The computational process is best illustrated by considering a simple first-order example: Minimize

$$J(x) = \int_0^T (x^2 + u^2)\, dt$$

subject to the constraint

$$\dot{x} = ax + u \qquad x_0 = c$$

$$|u| \leq 1{\cdot}0$$

where x, u are scalars.

Solution:

1. Take the interval $0 \to T$ and divide it into n subintervals, $T = n\Delta$. Let the range of u be divided into 2m so that $1 = m\delta$, u can vary between $\pm m\delta$. Divide the possible range of x into discrete values also, say $\ell\delta$; we have

$$J_n(x_0) = \min_{u_0, u_1, \cdots, u_{n-1}} \sum_{i=0}^{n-1} (x_i^2 + u_i^2)\Delta$$

$$= \min_{u_0} [(x_0^2 + u_0^2)\Delta + J_{n-1}(ax_0 + u_0)]$$

subject to the constraints

$$x_{i+1} = (ax_i + u_i)\Delta + x_i$$

$$|u| \leq m\delta$$

2. Now let us begin with a problem where x_T is not fixed. We shall start with the last term

$$J_1(x_{n-1}) = \min_{u_{n-1}} (x_{n-1}^2 + u_{n-1}^2)\Delta$$

Obviously, $u_{n-1} = 0$, hence, $J_1(x_{n-1}) = x_{n-1}^2$. Now we proceed to calculate

$$J_2(x_{n-2}) = \min_{u_{n-2}} [(x_{n-2}^2 + u_{n-2}^2)\Delta + J_1(x_{n-1})]$$

Here for every value x_{n-2}, we pick a control u_{n-2}. From the relation $x_{n-1} = x_{n-2} + (ax_{n-2} + u_{n-2})\Delta$ we get the corresponding x_{n-1} and $J_1(x_{n-1})$, looking through all possible u from $m\delta$ to $-m\delta$, we can determine $J_2(x_{n-2})$ and the corresponding optimal control u_{n-2}^0. We can enter them into Table 2.1.

Table 2.1. Dynamic Programming Solutions

x	$\frac{J_n(x_0)}{\Delta}$	u_0^0		$\frac{J_2(x_{n-2})}{\Delta}$	u_{n-2}^0	$\frac{J_1(x_{n-1})}{\Delta}$	u_{n-1}^0
$+\ell\delta$						$\ell\delta^2$	0
$+(\ell-1)\delta$						$[(\ell-1)\delta]^2$	0
⋮						⋮	
δ			Fill table			δ^2	⋮
0			from right			0	
$-\delta$			to left. ⟵			δ^2	
⋮						⋮	
$-(\ell-1)\delta$							
$-\ell\delta$						$\ell\delta^2$	0

Similarly, once the $J_2(x_{n-2})$, u^0_{n-2} columns of the table are filled, we can proceed to calculate $J_3(x_{n-3})$, u^0_{n-3}. Note that for each successive computation, only the last adjacent column of J's is needed. This is very advantageous from the computational standpoint.

3. After the complete table is filled out, we have the optimal solutions to not just one initial condition but all possible initial conditions from $+\ell\delta$ to $-\ell\delta$; hence, we really have a closed-loop control law. In other words, if the state variable x can be sensed, we can determine the optimal control u^0 immediately from Table 2.1. A numerical example is shown in Table 2.2 where $a = 0$, $\delta = \Delta = 1$, $m = 1$, $\ell = 5$, $n = 4$. Therefore, $x_{i+1} = x_i + u_i$ and

$$J_{4-i}(x_i) = \min_{u_i} [x_i^2 + u_i^2 + J_{4-i-1}(x_{i+1})]$$

Table 2.2. Numerical Solutions

x	$J_4(x_0)$	u_0^0	$J_3(x_1)$	u_1^0	$J_2(x_2)$	u_2^0	$J_1(x_3)$	u_3^0
5	57	-1	52	-1	42	-1	25	0
4	33	-1	31	-1	42	-1	16	0
3	17	-1	16	-1	14	-1	9	0
2	7	-1	7	-1	6	-1	4	0
1	2	-1	2	-1	2	-1	1	0
0	0	0	0	0	0	0	0	0
-1	2	1	2	1	2	1	1	0
-2	7	1	7	1	6	1	4	0
-3	17	1	16	1	14	1	9	0
-4	33	1	31	1	26	1	16	0
-5	57	1	52	1	32	1	25	0

From Table 2.2, we can obtain immediately the optimal cost frunction as well as the optimal-control law for any initial conditions from +5 to -5, for example, for $x_0 = 3$, $J_4(3) = 17$. The optimal control vector is $[-1, -1, -1, 0]$.

4. Two-point boundary-value problem: Now if the end point is fixed also, the problem actually becomes simpler since the $J_1(x_{n-1})$ and u_{n-1} are automatically fixed. In other words, for every state next to the last, there is only one control that will get it up to the final state. Since

$$x_n = x_{n-1} + (ax_{n-1} + u_{n-1})\Delta$$

Therefore,

$$u_{n-1} = \frac{x_n - x_{n-1}}{\Delta} - ax_{n-1}$$

for every x_{n-1}, u_{n-1} is fixed by these relations. From n-2 stage on, it is the same as initial value problem.[28] Note that if u is bounded, there are a limited number of states x_{n-1} allowable for the (n - 1)th stage, hence the table will grow like a Christmas tree as it proceeds to the left. To demonstrate this fact, let us use the previous numerical example. Now we require that $x_4 = 0$. We have the data from Table 2.3.

Table 2.3. Numerical Solutions (Fixed End Point)

x	$J_4(x_0)$	u_0^0	$J_3(x_1)$	u_1^0	$J_2(x_2)$	u_2^0	$J_1(x_3)$	u_3^0
5	-							
4	34	-1						
3	17	-1	17	-1				
2	7	-1	7	-1	7	-1		
1	2	-1	2	-1	2	-1	2	-1
0	0	0	0	0	0	0	0	0
-1	2	1	2	1	2	+1	2	1
-2	7	1	7	1	7	1		
-3	17	1	17	1				
-4	34	1						
-5	-							

Here, we see that $x_0 = 4$, the cost is 34, and the control is (-1, -1, -1, -1). For $x_0 = 5$, the solution does not exist for a 4-stage process.

The curse of dimensionality. In principle, the method of dynamic programming can solve all extremal problems. Furthermore, it will determine the global minimum or maximum as the case may be. Unfortunately, the method has one serious practical drawback. This is the so-called curse of dimensionality. Looking at our first-order example, we see that the solution requires a table of two dimensions. If we increase the order of the system by one, we will need a table of three dimensions. If we collapse it to two dimensions, we will need a table size of $[(2\ell)^2 \times 2n]$

instead of $2\ell \times 2n$. Obviously, the computer memory unit will soon be overwhelmed with further increase in the order of the system.

2.2.3 The Method of Gradients and Feasible Directions. The method of gradient, sometimes referred to as the method of steepest descent, is an elementary concept for the solution of extremal problems. It is an intuitively satisfying step-by-step procedure that solves the problem by asking three basic questions: (1) Which way? (2) How far? and (3) When to stop? As the name implies, this method seeks the information about the gradients and sets up a systematic procedure that provides the answers to these questions. To illustrate the basic idea, consider the simple example of a "hill-climbing" exercise in a dense fog. The objective is to climb as high as possible. Assuming no prior knowledge of the terrain, most participants will either consciously or subconsciously seek the answer to these three questions: (1) Which way? Pick the direction of the steepest local slope (local gradient); (2) How far to go? Go on that direction as long as you are going up; (3) When to stop? Stop when you get to a point where everywhere you go is down. Now, if we add a (inequality) constraint to the problem, say a stone wall, then we will proceed as usual until one comes to the wall. Since we cannot go through as the local slope dictates, then the next best thing (the feasible direction) is to go along the wall until we get to a point where everywhere we can go is down. Conceptually, this is the basic idea behind the method of the gradients and feasible directions.[55] As illustrated by this simple example, this method of hill climbing will always work. However, as long as our vision is limited, there is no way to tell if we are on a secondary peak or the highest peak. In other words, this method cannot tell the local extremum from the global extremum. This is the fundamental weakness of this method. The mathematical formulation of this method dates back to Cauchy (1847) and in a variational version to Hadamard (1908). Courant, Curry, Levenberg, and others have made various contributions and refinements. The application of this method to aerospace problems was introduced by Kelley,[32] and Bryson and his colleagues.[6] In what follows, a concise presentation is made on the application of the gradient method to the discrete version of extremal problems.

Consider a typical n-stage minimization problem where the dynamic specification is:

$$x_{i+1} = f(x_i, u_i, i) \qquad x_0 = c$$

$$u \in \Omega \text{ (some closed set)} \qquad u_i \text{ (scalar)}$$

The performance criterion is

$$\min_{u \in \Omega} J[x(0), u]$$

To start the problem, guess an initial control vector

$$\hat{u} = \begin{bmatrix} \hat{u}_0 \\ u_1 \\ \vdots \\ u_{n-1} \end{bmatrix}$$

and calculate the corresponding J. In general, this value of J is not the min J. We would like to find a systematic way of decreasing J by changing u so that in the limit it will approach the minimum. To do so, one uses the simple Taylor's series expansion.

$$\delta J = \nabla_u J \; \delta u + \text{higher order terms}$$

The procedure for solution is

1. Determine $\nabla_u J$.
2. Choose δu to be in opposite direction to $\nabla_u J$, say $\delta u = -\beta(\nabla_u J)'$ where β = some constant; this assures δJ to be negative.
3. Choose a new control $\hat{u}_{new} = \hat{u}_{old} + \delta u$.
4. Repeat the procedures 1 to 3.
5. Stop when $\nabla_u J \to 0$ or when all the controls are on the boundary so that no further improvements are possible.

The procedure listed here appears very straightforward, however, the mechanics of computation itself is rather involved. First of all, the relation of J and u is often very complicated. Hence, $\nabla_u J$ cannot be evaluated easily. Secondly, the choice of β is not a simple matter, since a too large β will invalidate the simple first-term approximation of this Taylor's series expansion. On the other hand, a too small β slows down the convergence of the problem. The optimal choice (or happy compromise) of β is often an art, dependent on the skill of the programmer.

In what follows, a typical application of this concept will be presented. This method was first introduced by Ho.[18, 22] The basic technique is developed for linear systems. However, it can be readily extended to nonlinear systems by using the perturbation equations. To demonstrate the fundamental ideas, a simple linear stationary single-input system is considered:

1. Plant:

$$x(i+1) = \Phi x(i) + \Gamma u_i \qquad x_0 = c$$

where x, Γ are $n \times 1$; Φ is $n \times n$ and $i = 0, 1, \cdots, k-1$.

2. Performance criterion: Minimize the generalized terminal norm

$$J = \|x(k)\|_R^2$$

where R = some positive definite matrix.

3. Constraints:

$$|u_i(t)| \leq 1$$

for all i.

Solution:

1. Determine $\nabla_u J$

$$\nabla_u J = \nabla_{x(k)} J \frac{\partial x(k)}{\partial u}$$

$$= 2x(k)'RG$$

where

$$G \triangleq \frac{\partial x(k)}{\partial u}$$

and is $n \times k$. Once an initial control vector $\hat{u}$ is selected, then $x(k)'$ is specified and R is given, therefore the problem is reduced to evaluation of G.

$$G \triangleq \begin{bmatrix} \frac{\partial x_1(k)}{\partial u_0} & \frac{\partial x_1(k)}{\partial u_1} & \cdots & \frac{\partial x_1(k)}{\partial u_{k-1}} \\ \vdots & \vdots & & \vdots \\ \frac{\partial x_n(k)}{\partial u_0} & \frac{\partial x_n(k)}{\partial u_1} & \cdots & \frac{\partial x_n(k)}{\partial u_{k-1}} \end{bmatrix}$$

The columns of G are the partials of $x(k)$ with respect to the initial control $u_0, u_1, \cdots, u_{k-1}$.

In the continuous case, this type of information can in general be obtained by using the adjoint equation. In the stationary discrete case, this is very easy to obtain.

From the dynamic equations given, we have

$$x(1) = \Phi x(0) + \Gamma u_0$$

$$x(2) = \Phi x(1) + \Gamma u_1 = \Phi^2 x(0) + \Phi\Gamma u_0 + \Gamma u_1$$

$$\vdots$$

$$x(k) = \Phi^k x(0) + \Phi^{k-1}\Gamma u_0 + \Phi^{k-2}\Gamma u_1 + \cdots + \Gamma u_{k-1}$$

Therefore,

$$\frac{\partial x(k)}{\partial u_0} = \Phi^{k-1}\Gamma, \ \frac{\partial x(k)}{\partial u_1} = \Phi^{k-2}\Gamma, \ \cdots, \frac{\partial x_k}{\partial u_{k-1}} = \Gamma$$

and, therefore,

$$G = \left[\Phi^{k-1}\Gamma \mid \Phi^{k-2}\Gamma \mid \cdots \mid \Phi\Gamma \mid \Gamma \right]$$

Once G is determined, we can calculate $\nabla_u J$. To obtain the vector δu, Ho[22] suggests the following technique: Let $\delta u = \beta v$ where β is a scalar, v a vector, and where the elements of the vector v are

$$v_j = \begin{cases} 1 - \hat{u}_j & \text{if } -\dfrac{\partial J}{\partial u_j} > 1 - \hat{u}_j \\ -\dfrac{\partial J}{\partial u_j} & \text{if } -1 - \hat{u}_j \le -\dfrac{\partial J}{\partial u_j} \le (1 - \hat{u}_j) \\ -1 - \hat{u}_j & \text{if } -\dfrac{\partial J}{\partial u_j} < -1 - \hat{u}_j \end{cases}$$

where $j = 0, 1, \cdots, k-1$ and β is defined as†

$$\beta = \text{sat}\left[-\frac{\nabla_u J v}{2v' G' R G v} \right]$$

where

$$\text{sat}(\alpha) \triangleq \begin{cases} \alpha & \text{if } |\alpha| < 1 \\ \pm 1 & \text{if } |\alpha| \ge 1 \end{cases}$$

---

†The expression for β is obtained by maximizing the series expansion including the second-order term; $\delta J = \nabla_u J\, \delta u + \delta u'\, G'RG\, \delta u + \cdots = \beta \nabla_u J v + \beta^2 v' G' R G v + \cdots$ with respect to β.

Once δu is determined, a new control vector $\hat{u}_{new} = \hat{u}_{old} + \delta u$ is produced and the whole procedure is repeated until $\delta u \rightarrow \epsilon$ where ϵ is a very small quantity. With slight modifications, this technique can be easily generalized to the case with state variable constraints.[19, 22] This technique can be extended to solve nonlinear systems also. In the nonlinear case, once an initial set of controls is chosen, we obtain a specific trajectory. Using the perturbation equations about this nominal trajectory, we obtain a set of linear equations, and hence the whole procedure can be applied. Once δu is obtained, a new reference trajectory is generated and the process can be repeated.

2.2.4. Summary. In this second part of Chapter 2, the basic concepts of three numerical methods for obtaining the solutions to extremal problems are presented. It was shown that the solution to the two-point boundary-value problem is in general quite difficult, especially when subjected to inequality constraints. The dynamic programming approach on the other hand is quite straight forward conceptually and can be used, in principle, to solve all extremal problems. Further, once the problem is solved, we have (1) the global extremum and (2) an optimal policy for all possible initial conditions (a closed-loop solution). The unfortunate drawback of this technique is the so-called "curse of dimensionality" which limits its application to simple systems. The method of the gradient is a successive approximation procedure that if handled properly will converge to the extremal. This method is conceptually very simple and is currently quite popular. One of the basic drawbacks of this technique is that it may converge to a local extremal. This drawback can be overcome in practice either by physical insight of the system or by the time-consuming process of picking many initial guesses in $\hat{u}$ and seeing if it converges to the same solution. The drawbacks of the various methods mentioned are inherent but not absolute. In most cases, they can be overcome with ingenuity and experience. For the sake of clarity, the gradient technique has been simplified by using only ordinary calculus. If we desire to use calculus of variation, we must introduce the influence function (Green's function); however, the basic concept is the same. Excellent references on this subject are References 7, 10, 13, 33, 39, and 53. Finally, it should be pointed out that there are numerous extensions and modifications of these basic concepts as well as other computation methods in the literature. They will not be discussed here because of space limitations.

Chapter 3

OPTIMAL ESTIMATION

In this chapter, we deal with the problem of optimal smoothing, filtering, and prediction. These are the fundamental estimation problems in a stochastic environment. In the general problem of control and communication, we wish (1) to obtain the means to separate the signal from the noise and (2) to predict the random signal or both. One of the most significant results in this problem area is the pioneering work by Wiener, who showed that the problems 1 and 2 lead to the famous Wiener-Hopf integral equation and demonstrated the solution for the case of stationary statistics and rational spectra. Since Wiener's work, numerous extensions and generalizations followed. Most of the work has been done in the frequency domain with the objective to obtain the optimal linear dynamic system that is the solution to problem 1 or 2 namely the "Wiener-filter." In 1960, Kalman[26] treated the filtering problem in the time domain from the "state" point of view. He showed that the solution of the optimal filter can be characterized by a set of differential equations. His results are generally referred to as the Kalman filter or the Wiener-Kalman filter. In this chapter, we shall first review the basic concepts of the Wiener filter and then proceed to discuss the Kalman filter. A discrete version of the Kalman filter is derived by using ordinary calculus. The general method of the "least-squares" fit is discussed, and it is shown that its result for the dynamic case is the same as that of the Kalman filter. The classical method of maximum-likelihood estimation by Fisher is also introduced. It is shown that in linear systems with Gaussian inputs the problem is reduced to that of the simple "least-squares fit." Finally, the Bayesian approach to stochastic estimation[23] is discussed. The latter presents a unified approach to stochastic estimation. It is the author's opinion that the Bayesian approach offers considerable advantage in clarifying the basic concepts of estimation theory; it is shown that the Kalman filter can be readily derived, further it can be extended to nonlinear and non-Gaussian cases.

3.1 The Wiener Filter

In this section, the basic Wiener filter will be derived and discussed. The basic theory behind the Wiener filter is well known and is presented in detail in many books such as References 12,

35, 38, and so forth. The objective here is not to rederive it in its entirety but rather to point out the basic concepts and its relation with the material to be presented in subsequent sections.

Given: 1. A set of signals and noise-stationary random processes with known statistical characteristics.
2. Desired output of the system x(t) expressed as the output of a linear invariant (not necessarily physically realizable) filter, operating on the signal.
3. The criterion for optimality: min $E[\tilde{x}^2]$ where $\tilde{x}(t) \triangleq$ filter output - desired output $= \hat{x}(t) - x(t)$.

Problem: Find a linear invariant physically realizable filter that will operate on (1) and minimize $E[\tilde{x}^2]$ as in Figure 3.1.

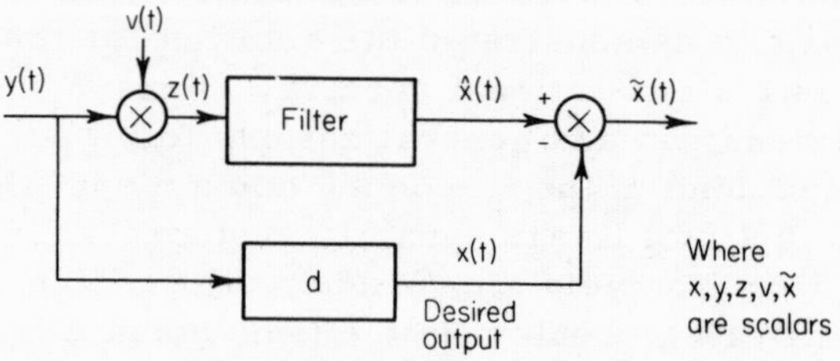

Figure 3.1. Block diagram for optimal filtering problem.

Solution: Let $w_F(t)$ be the weighting function of the filter and $w_d(t)$ be the weighting function of the desired model d. From the basic theory of linear systems, we have

$$\hat{x}(t) = \int_{-\infty}^{\infty} w_F(\tau)\, z(t-\tau)\, d\tau \tag{3.1}$$

for simplicity, let

$$w_d(t) = 1$$

so that

$$x(t) = y(t)$$

therefore,

$$\tilde{x}(t) = \hat{x}(t) - x(t)$$

$$\overline{\tilde{x}^2(t)} = \overline{\hat{x}(t)^2} - \overline{2\hat{x}(t)x(t)} + \overline{x(t)^2} \tag{3.2}$$

$$\hat{x}(t)^2 = \int_{-\infty}^{\infty} w_F(\tau_1) z(t - \tau_1)\, d\tau_1 \int_{-\infty}^{\infty} w_F(\tau_2) z(t - \tau_2)\, d\tau_2$$

$$\overline{\hat{x}(t)^2} = \int_{-\infty}^{\infty} d\tau_1\, w_F(\tau_1) \int_{-\infty}^{\infty} d\tau_2\, w_F(\tau_2)\, \overline{z(t - \tau_1) z(t - \tau_2)}$$

$$= \int_{-\infty}^{\infty} d\tau_1\, w_F(\tau_1) \int_{-\infty}^{\infty} d\tau_2\, w_F(\tau_2)\, \phi_{zz}(\tau_1 - \tau_2) \tag{3.3}$$

$$\overline{\hat{x}(t) x(t)} = \int_{-\infty}^{\infty} d\tau_1\, w_F(\tau_1)\, \overline{z(t - \tau_1) y(t)}$$

$$= \int_{-\infty}^{\infty} d\tau_1\, w_F(\tau_1)\, \phi_{zy}(\tau_1) \tag{3.4}$$

$$\overline{x(t)^2} = \overline{y(t)^2} \tag{3.5}$$

Now the problem becomes that of finding $w_F(t)$ that will minimize

$$\overline{\tilde{x}^2} = \overline{\hat{x}(t)^2} - 2\overline{\hat{x}(t) x(t)} + \overline{x(t)^2}$$

(Note that $\overline{x(t)^2}$ is not a function of $w_F(t)$.) This problem fits neatly into the basic framework of classical calculus of variation. To solve the problem, let

$$w_F(t) = w_{F_0}(t) + \epsilon\, w(t)$$

where $w_{F_0}(t)$ is the desired solution. Then the necessary condition for minimum is

$$\left. \frac{\partial \overline{\tilde{x}^2}}{\partial \epsilon} \right|_{\epsilon = 0} = 0$$

$$\frac{\partial \overline{\tilde{x}(t)^2}}{\partial \epsilon} = \frac{\partial \overline{\hat{x}(t)^2}}{\partial \epsilon} - \frac{2\, \partial \overline{\hat{x}(t) x(t)}}{\partial \epsilon} \tag{3.6}$$

$$\frac{\partial \overline{\hat{x}(t)^2}}{\partial \epsilon} = 2 \int_{-\infty}^{\infty} d\tau_1\, w(\tau_1) \int_{-\infty}^{\infty} d\tau_2\, w_{F_0}(\tau_2)\, \phi_{zz}(\tau_1 - \tau_2)$$

$$+\, \epsilon \text{ (higher order terms)} \tag{3.7}$$

$$2\frac{\partial}{\partial\epsilon}\overline{\hat{x}(t)x(t)} = 2\int_{-\infty}^{\infty} d\tau_1\ w(\tau_1)\ \phi_{zy}(\tau_1) \tag{3.8}$$

Setting

$$\left.\frac{d\overline{\tilde{x}^2}}{d\epsilon}\right|_{\epsilon=0} = 0$$

we have

$$\int_{-\infty}^{\infty} d\tau_1\ w(\tau_1)\left[\int_{-\infty}^{\infty} d\tau\ \ w_{F_0}(\tau)\ \phi_{zz}(\tau_1 - \tau) - \phi_{zy}(\tau_1)\right] = 0 \tag{3.9}$$

Since w(t) is arbitrary, (for $t \geq 0$ but zero for $t < 0$) the necessary condition for minimum becomes (Note: t and τ_1 are interchanged here.)

$$\int_{-\infty}^{\infty} d\tau\ w_{F_0}(\tau)\ \phi_{zz}(t - \tau) - \phi_{zy}(t) = 0 \qquad t \geq 0 \tag{3.10}$$

This is the famous Wiener-Hopf equation. Here the necessary condition for optimality appears as an integral equation, the solution is not a trivial task. To find $w_{F_0}(t)$, we usually have to use integral transform techniques and solve the problem in the frequency domain.

3.2 The Wiener-Kalman Filter

In the foregoing section, it was shown that the optimal (Wiener) filter is characterized by an integral equation (the Wiener-Hopf equation). In this section, we look at the problem in the time domain using the so-called state point of view. Here we characterize the driving signal by the output of a linear dynamic system driven by white noise. There is no loss of generality since, in the previous case, either the autocorrelation function or the power-density function must be given. If the spectrum is rational, it can always be represented as the output of a linear system driven by white noise. In what follows, we shall formulate the problem in a manner similar to that given by Kalman in References 26, 30, and 31. See Figure 3.2.

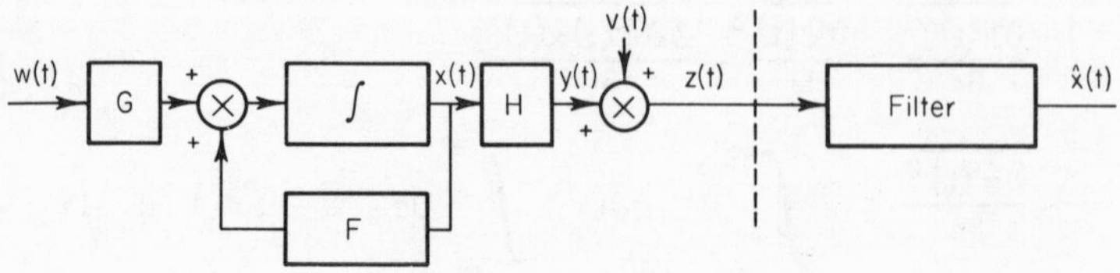

Figure 3.2. Problem formulation of the Wiener-Kalman filter.

Problem:
Basic model:

$$\left.\begin{aligned} \frac{dx}{dt} &= F(t)x(t) + G(t)w(t) \\ z(t) &= y(t) + v(t) = H(t)x(t) + v(t) \end{aligned}\right\} \tag{3.11}$$

where w(t), v(t) are white Gaussian noises

$$E[w(t)] = E[v(t)] = 0$$

$$E[w(t)w(\tau)] = Q(t)\delta(t - \tau)$$

$$E[v(t)v(\tau)] = R(t)\delta(t - \tau)$$

Now given measurements z(t) up to t find a linear operator $\hat{x}(t_1|t)$ at time t_1 that has the properties:

1. $E[\hat{x}(t_1|t)] = E[x(t_1)]$
2. $E\,||\tilde{x}(t_1|t)||_B^2 = \min$

where B is any nonnegative definite matrix in which

$$\tilde{x}(t_1|t) \triangleq x(t_1) - \hat{x}(t_1|t)$$

In other words, $\hat{x}(t_1|t)$ is to be an unbiased minimum variance estimator of $x(t_1)$. Note that we have if $t_1 < t$ the smoothing problem, if $t_1 = t$ the filtering problem, if $t_1 > t$ the optimum prediction problem.

Solution: In References 26, 30, and 31 Kalman showed that the solution to the optimum filtering problem is the output of a similar dynamic system.

$$\frac{d\hat{x}(t|t)}{dt} = F(t)\,\hat{x}(t|t) + k(t)\,[z(t) - H(t)\hat{x}(t|t)] \tag{3.12}$$

where

$$k(t) \triangleq P(t)H'(t)\,R^{-1}(t) \tag{3.13}$$

and

$$P(t) \triangleq E[\tilde{x}(t|t)\,\tilde{x}(t|t)']$$

is the covariance matrix, and is given by the differential equation

$$\frac{dP(t)}{dt} = F(t)\,P(t) + P(t)'F'(t) - P(t)\,H'(t)\,R^{-1}(t)\,H(t)\,P(t) + G(t)\,Q(t)\,G(t)' \qquad (3.14)$$

This variance equation is often referred to as the matrix Ricatti equation. The block diagram of the Kalman filter is shown in Figure 3.3. The exact derivation of the Kalman filter is rather

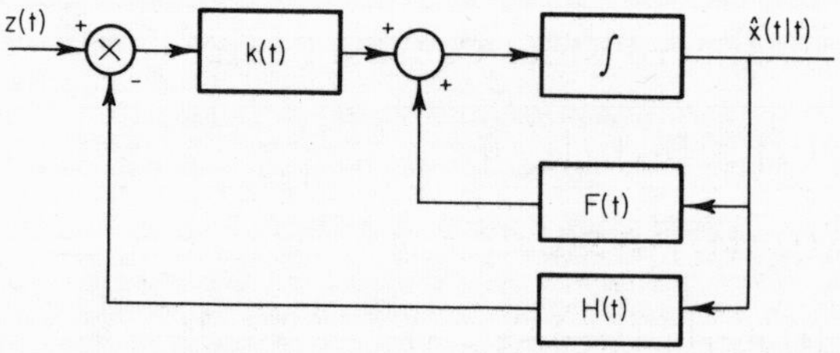

Figure 3.3. Block diagram of the Kalman filter.

involved† and hence will not be repeated here. The interested reader may consult References 26, 30, and 31 for the details. However, since in this thesis our emphasis is on digital computation, we shall attempt to derive the Kalman filter in its discrete equivalent form in Section 3.3. At this point, it is noteworthy to point out that in the stationary case where F, G, H are time invariant, the covariance matrix will converge to a constant, hence K is a constant in the steady state, therefore the optimal filter is also time invariant and is given by

$$\frac{d\hat{x}(t)}{dt} = [F - kH]\hat{x}(t) + kz(t) \qquad (3.15)$$

this is the time domain equivalent of the Wiener filter given in the frequency domain by solving the Wiener-Hopf integral equation.

3.3 The Wiener-Kalman Filter (The Discrete Case)

The discrete version of the Wiener-Kalman filter was first presented by Kalman[26] in 1960. In 1961, similar results were independently derived by Battin[3] where he obtained the optimal linear estimator for both correlated and uncorrelated measure-

---

†Kalman employs the method of orthogonal projections to derive his results; since this concept is rather unfamiliar to most engineers, it will not be discussed here. The author feels that the "Bayesian approach," to be discussed later, is a far more straightforward way of getting the same results.

ment errors. Battin first assumes that the solution is of the form of a recursive relation, where the new estimate is the sum of the extrapolated estimate, based on past estimates, and a weighting matrix modifying the residues (new measurement — extrapolated measurement). Then, the problem becomes that of finding the optimum weighting matrix so as to minimize the mean-square error of the estimates. In the following, we will formulate the problem as a classical optimization problem similar to that of Bryson and Ho.[8, 9, 20] We will show that the optimal filtering solution could be obtained via ordinary calculus, further, recursive optimal smoothing solutions could also be obtained. This derivation proceeds as follows: Consider the dynamic relationship

$$\left.\begin{aligned} x_{k+1} &= \Phi x_k + \Gamma w_k \\ z_k &= H x_k + v_k \end{aligned}\right\} \tag{3.16}$$

where w_k, v_k are independent Gaussian random sequences with zero mean and covariance matrix Q, R, respectively. The initial condition is $x(0)$ where $E(x_0) = \overline{x}$ and $E[(x_0 - \overline{x})(x_0 - \overline{x})'] = P_0$ and Φ, Γ, H may be time varying. See Figure 3.4.

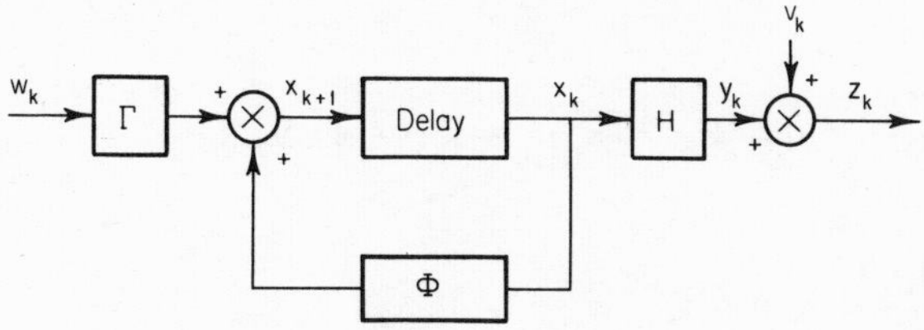

Figure 3.4. Model of signal source.

Problem: Given measurements $z_1, z_2, \cdots, z_n$ determine the best estimate of states x_i, $0 \leq i \leq n$ in some sense. We call these estimates $\hat{x}_{i|n}$. Obviously, there are many ways of specifying a criterion that defines the optimal estimate. In this section, we assume that the filter which produces the estimate is of the form of Figure 3.5, where $\hat{w}_{i|n}$ and $\hat{x}_{i|n}$

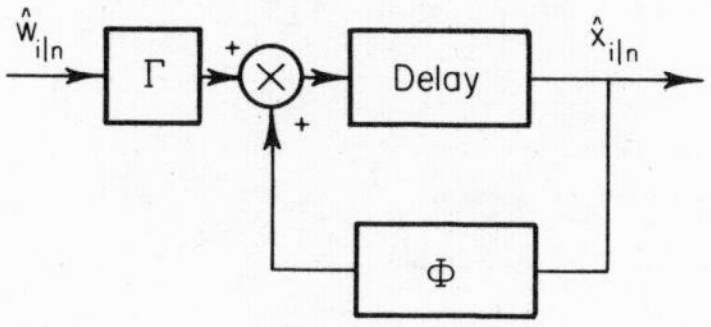

Figure 3.5. Model of the optimal filter.

are related to the measurements $z_1, z_2, \cdots, z_n$ in such a way that they are the minimum variance estimates. To be more specific, we define our problem as follows: Given measurements $z_1, z_2, \cdots, z_n$ determine the estimates $\hat{x}_{i|n}$ for $0 \leq i \leq n$ that minimizes the criterion.

$$J = \frac{1}{2} ||\hat{x}_{0|n} - \bar{x}||^2_{P_0^{-1}} + \sum_{i=0}^{n-1} \frac{1}{2} \left[|| z_{i+1} - H\hat{x}_{i+1|n}||^2_{R^{-1}} + ||\hat{w}_{i|n}||^2_{Q^{-1}} \right] \tag{3.17}$$

subject to the constraints

$$\hat{x}_{i+1|n} = \Phi\hat{x}_{i|n} + \Gamma\hat{w}_{i|n} \tag{3.18}$$

Solution: Define a set of multiplier vectors $\lambda_0, \lambda_1, \cdots, \lambda_n$ and a new function,

$$J* = J + \sum_{i=0}^{n-1} < \lambda_i \cdot \left(\hat{x}_{i+1|n} - \Phi\hat{x}_{i|n} - \Gamma\hat{w}_{i|n} \right) >$$

This is simply a multidimensional algebriac minimization problem the solution is as follows:

$$\left\{ \begin{aligned} \frac{\partial J*'}{\partial \hat{x}_{0|n}} &= 0 = P_0^{-1} [\hat{x}_{0|n} - \bar{x}] - \Phi' \lambda_0 \\ \frac{\partial J*'}{\partial \hat{w}_{0|n}} &= 0 = Q^{-1} \hat{w}_{0|n} - \Gamma'\lambda_0 \\ \frac{\partial J*'}{\partial \lambda_0} &= 0 = \hat{x}_{i|n} - \Phi\hat{x}_{0|n} - \Gamma\hat{w}_{0|n} \end{aligned} \right.$$

$$\left\{ \begin{aligned} \frac{\partial J*'}{\partial \hat{x}_{1|n}} &= 0 = H' R^{-1} H\hat{x}_{1|n} - H'R^{-1} z_1 + \lambda_0 - \Phi'\lambda_1 \\ \frac{\partial J*'}{\partial \hat{w}_{1|n}} &= 0 = Q^{-1} \hat{w}_{1|n} - \Gamma'\lambda_1 \\ \frac{\partial J*'}{\partial \lambda_1} &= 0 = \hat{x}_{2|n} - \Phi\hat{x}_{1|n} - \Gamma\hat{w}_{1|n} \end{aligned} \right.$$

$$\vdots$$

$$\left\{\begin{aligned} &\frac{\partial J^{*\prime}}{\partial \hat{x}_{n-1|n}} = 0 = H'R^{-1}H\hat{x}_{n-1|n} - H'R^{-1}z_{n-1} + \lambda_{n-2} - \Phi'\lambda_{n-1} \\ &\frac{\partial J^{*\prime}}{\partial \hat{w}_{n-1|n}} = 0 = Q^{-1}\hat{w}_{n-1|n} - \Gamma'\lambda_{n-1} \\ &\frac{\partial J^{*\prime}}{\partial \lambda_{n-1}} = 0 = \hat{x}_n - \Phi\hat{x}_{n-1|n} - \Gamma\hat{w}_{n-1|n} \end{aligned}\right.$$

$$\frac{\partial J^{*\prime}}{\partial x_n} = H'R^{-1}H\hat{x}_{n|n} - H'R^{-1}z_n + \lambda_{n-1} = 0$$

Combining and rearranging, we have the following relationships:

$$\hat{w}_{i|n} = Q\Gamma'\lambda_i \tag{3.19}$$

$$\hat{x}_{0|n} = P_0\Phi'\lambda_0 + \overline{x} \qquad \overline{x} = \hat{x}_{0|0} \tag{3.20}$$

$$\hat{x}_{i+1|n} = \Phi\hat{x}_{i|n} + \Gamma Q\Gamma'\lambda_i \tag{3.21}$$

$$\lambda_i = \Phi'\lambda_{i+1} + H'R^{-1}\left[z_{i+1} - H\hat{x}_{i+1|n}\right] \tag{3.22}$$

$$\lambda_n = 0$$

$$i = 0, 1, 2, \cdots, n$$

Here we see that the solution to the smoothing problem is characterized by a two-point boundary-value problem (TPBVP). In the continuous case, these are differential equations in contrast to the Wiener-Hopf integral equations. In general, these TPBVP are not easily solved.

3.3.1 Optimal Filtering. Now we shall consider the case where we are interested only in the filtering problem, that is, we wish to obtain the best estimate $\hat{x}_{i|i} \triangleq \hat{x}(i)|z_i, z_{i-1}, \cdots, z_1$. To solve this problem, we shall treat the two-point boundary-value problem in successive steps and try to develop a recursive relationship that relates the new estimate to the old estimate and the new measurement. We shall begin by letting n = 1, then the TPBVP becomes

$$\lambda_1 = 0$$

$$\hat{x}_{1|1} = \Phi\hat{x}_{0|1} + \Gamma Q\Gamma'\lambda_0 = [\Phi P_0 \Phi' + PQ\Gamma']\lambda_0 + \Phi\bar{x}$$

$$= P_{1|0}\lambda_0 + \Phi\bar{x} = P_{1|0}H'R^{-1}[z_1 - H\hat{x}_{1|1}] + \Phi\bar{x}$$

Therefore,

$$[I + P_{1|0}H'R^{-1}H]\,\hat{x}_{1|1} = P_{1|0}H'R^{-1}z_1 + \Phi\bar{x}$$

and

$$\hat{x}_{1|1} = [P_{1|0}{}^{-1} + H'R^{-1}H]^{-1}H'R^{-1}z_1 + [P_{1|0}{}^{-1} + H'R^{-1}H]^{-1}P_{1|0}{}^{-1}\,\Phi\bar{x}$$

$$= P_{1|1}H'R^{-1}[z_1 - H\Phi\bar{x}] + \Phi\bar{x} \tag{3.23}$$

where

$$\bar{x} \triangleq \hat{x}_{0|0}$$

$$P_{1|1} \triangleq [P_{1|0}{}^{-1} + H'R^{-1}H]^{-1}$$

$$= P_{1|0} - P_{1|0}H'(HP_{1|0}H' + R)^{-1}HP_{1|0} \tag{3.24}$$

(matrix inversion lemma)

$$P_{1|0} \triangleq \Phi P_{0|0}\Phi' + \Gamma Q\Gamma'$$

Now try n = 2. The TPBVP is

$$\lambda_2 = 0$$

for Equation 3.21,

$$\hat{x}_{2|2} = \Phi\hat{x}_{1|2} + \Gamma Q\Gamma'\lambda_1 \tag{3.25}$$

for Equation 3.20,

$$\hat{x}_{1|2} = P_{1|0}\lambda_0 + \Phi\bar{x} \tag{3.26}$$

and from Equation 3.22

$$\lambda_1 = H'R^{-1}[z_2 - H\hat{x}_{2|2}] \tag{3.27}$$

$$\lambda_0 = \Phi'\lambda_1 + H'R^{-1}[z_1 - H\hat{x}_{1|2}] \tag{3.28}$$

Since we want $\hat{x}_{2|2}$ to be a function of $\hat{x}_{1|1}$, we substitute Equation 3.23 into Equation 3.28. Therefore,

$$\lambda_0 = \Phi'\lambda_1 + P_{1|1}^{-1}\hat{x}_{1|1} - H'R^{-1}H\,\hat{x}_{1|2} \qquad (3.29)$$

Substituting Equation 3.29 into Equation 3.26, we have

$$\hat{x}_{1|2} = P_{1|0}[\Phi'\lambda_1 + P_{1|1}^{-1}\hat{x}_{1|1} - H'R^{-1}H\,\hat{x}_{1|2}]$$

and solving this equation, we have

$$\hat{x}_{1|2} = P_{1|1}\Phi'\lambda_1 + \hat{x}_{1|1} \qquad (3.30)$$

Substitute Equation 3.30 into Equation 3.25,

$$\hat{x}_{2|2} = [\Phi P_{1|1}\Phi' + \Gamma Q\Gamma']\lambda_1 + \Phi\hat{x}_{1|1}$$

$$= P_{2|1}\lambda_1 + \Phi\hat{x}_{1|1}$$

$$= P_{2|1}H'R^{-1}[z_2 - H\hat{x}_{2|2}] + \Phi\hat{x}_{1|1}$$

Rearranging, we have

$$\hat{x}_{2|2} = P_{2|2}H'R^{-1}z_2 - P_{2|2}P_{2|1}^{-1}\Phi\hat{x}_{1|1}$$

$$= P_{2|2}H'R^{-1}[z_2 - H\Phi\hat{x}_{1|1}] + P_{2|2}P_{2|1}^{-1}\Phi\hat{x}_{1|1} + P_{2|2}H'R^{-1}H\Phi\hat{x}_{1|1}$$

$$= P_{2|2}H'R^{-1}[z_2 - H\Phi\hat{x}_{1|1}] + P_{2|2}[P_{2|1}^{-1} + H'R^{-1}H]\,\Phi\hat{x}_{1|1}$$

$$= \Phi\hat{x}_{1|1} + P_{2|2}H'R^{-1}[z_2 - H\Phi\hat{x}_{1|1}] \qquad (3.31)$$

where

$$P_{2|2} \triangleq [P_{2|1}^{-1} + H'R^{-1}H]^{-1}$$

Summarizing, we have

$$\hat{x}_{2|2} = \Phi\hat{x}_{1|1} + P_{2|2}H'R^{-1}[z_2 - H\Phi\hat{x}_{1|1}]$$

$$P_{2|1} \triangleq \Phi P_{1|1}\Phi' + \Gamma Q\Gamma'$$

$$P_{2|2} \triangleq [P_{2|1}^{-1} + H'R^{-1}H]^{-1}$$

$$= P_{2|1} - P_{2|1}H'[HP_{2|1}H' + R]^{-1}HP_{2|1} \tag{3.32}$$

Proceeding in this manner for n = 3, 4, $\cdots$, we can show that the recursive relationship 3.32 holds for all n, therefore in general, we have

$$\left.\begin{aligned}
\hat{x}_{n|n} &= \Phi\hat{x}_{n-1|n-1} + P_{n|n}H'R^{-1}[z_n - H\Phi\hat{x}_{n-1|n-1}] \\
P_{n|n-1} &= \Phi P_{n-1|n-1}\Phi' + \Gamma Q\Gamma' \\
P_{n|n} &= [P_{n|n-1}^{-1} + H'R^{-1}H]^{-1} \\
&= P_{n|n-1} - P_{n|n-1}H'[HP_{n|n-1}H' + R]^{-1}HP_{n|n-1}
\end{aligned}\right\} \tag{3.33}$$

The relationships (Equations 3.33) are precisely the discrete equivalent of the Kalman filter, if we consider $P_{n|n}$ as the covariance matrix of $x_{n|n}$, and $P_{n|n-1}$ as the covariance matrix of $x_{n|n-1}$.

3.3.2 The Optimal Smoothing Solution. In Section 3.3.1, it was shown that the optimal solution to the criterion of Equation 3.17 subjected to the constraints Equation 3.18 is characterized by a set of two-point boundary-value problems (Equations 3.19 through 3.23). Solving this set of two-point boundary problems, we obtain all of the optimal smoothing solutions $\hat{x}_{n-1|n}, \hat{x}_{n-2|n}, \hat{x}_{n-3|n}, \cdots, \hat{x}_{1|n}, \hat{x}_{0|n}$. If we take on an extra measurement, say z_{n+1}, we will have to solve a new set of TPBVP. In practice, this is very inefficient, since it is often difficult and laborious to solve a TPBVP, especially in real time. In Section 3.3.1, it was shown that the optimal filtering solution could be obtained via a neat recursive relationship (Equation 3.33), where the new estimate $\hat{x}_{n+1|n+1}$ is given as a linear function of the old estimate $\hat{x}_{n|n}$ and the residue involving the new measurement. In this section, we will derive a set of recursive relations for the optimal smoothing solutions for the same problem. Here we will start by assuming that the optimal filtering solution $\hat{x}_{n|n}$ is known and then work backward to get $\hat{x}_{i|n}$ for all $i < n$ using the constraint equation (Equation 3.18). The detailed derivation is as follows: From the basic constraint equation, Equation 3.18, we have

$$\hat{x}_{n|n} = \Phi\hat{x}_{n-1|n} + \Gamma\hat{w}_{n-1|n} \tag{3.34}$$

From Equations 3.19 and 3.22, we have

$$\left.\begin{aligned} \hat{w}_{n-1|n} &= Q\Gamma'\lambda_{n-1} \\ \lambda_{n-1} &= H'R^{-1}[z_n - H\hat{x}_{n|n}] \end{aligned}\right\} \tag{3.35}$$

Substituting Equation 3.35 into 3.34, we have

$$\hat{x}_{n|n} = \Phi\hat{x}_{n-1|n} + \Gamma Q\Gamma' H'R^{-1}[z_n - H\hat{x}_{n|n}] \tag{3.36}$$

From Equation 3.33, we have

$$\hat{x}_{n|n} = \Phi\hat{x}_{n-1|n-1} + P_{n|n}H'R^{-1}[z_n - H\Phi\hat{x}_{n-1|n-1}] \tag{3.37}$$

Substituting into Equation 3.36, we have

$$\begin{aligned} \hat{x}_{n|n} = \Phi\hat{x}_{n-1|n} + \Gamma Q\Gamma' H'R^{-1}\{z_n &- H\Phi\hat{x}_{n-1|n-1} \\ &- HP_{n|n}H'R^{-1}[z_n - H\Phi\hat{x}_{n-1|n-1}]\} \end{aligned}$$

Rearranging, we obtain

$$\begin{aligned} \Phi\hat{x}_{n-1|n} &= \hat{x}_{n|n} - \Gamma Q\Gamma'[P_{n|n}^{-1} - H'R^{-1}H]P_{n|n}H'R^{-1}[z_n - H\Phi\hat{x}_{n-1|n-1}] \\ &= \hat{x}_{n|n} - \Gamma Q\Gamma'[P_n^{-1} - H'R^{-1}H][\hat{x}_{n|n} - \Phi\hat{x}_{n-1|n-1}] \\ &= \Phi\hat{x}_{n-1|n-1} + \hat{x}_{n|n} - \Phi\hat{x}_{n-1|n-1} - \Gamma Q\Gamma'[P_{n|n-1}^{-1}][\hat{x}_{n|n} - \Phi\hat{x}_{n-1|n-1}] \\ &= \Phi\hat{x}_{n-1|n-1} + [I - \Gamma Q\Gamma'(P_{n|n-1}^{-1})][\hat{x}_{n|n} - \Phi\hat{x}_{n-1|n-1}] \\ &= \Phi\hat{x}_{n-1|n-1} + [P_{n|n-1} - \Gamma Q\Gamma']P_{n|n-1}^{-1}[\hat{x}_{n|n} - \Phi\hat{x}_{n-1|n-1}] \\ &= \Phi\hat{x}_{n-1|n-1} + [\Phi P_{n-1|n-1}\Phi']P_{n|n-1}^{-1}[\hat{x}_{n|n} - \Phi\hat{x}_{n-1|n-1}] \end{aligned}$$

Therefore,

$$\hat{x}_{n-1|n} = \hat{x}_{n-1|n-1} + P_{n-1|n-1}\Phi' P_{n|n-1}^{-1}[\hat{x}_{n|n} - \Phi\hat{x}_{n-1|n-1}] \tag{3.38}$$

Proceeding to the case n - 2 and using the relations 3.19, 3.21, 3.28, and 3.33, we have

$$
\begin{aligned}
\Phi\hat{x}_{n-2|n} &= \hat{x}_{n-1|n} - \Gamma\hat{w}_{n-2|n} \\
&= \hat{x}_{n-1|n} - \Gamma Q\Gamma'[\Phi'\lambda_{n-1} + H'R^{-1}(z_{n-1} - H\hat{x}_{n-1|n})] \\
&= \hat{x}_{n-1|n} - \Gamma Q\Gamma'\{\Phi'H'R^{-1}[z_n - H\hat{x}_{n|n}] \\
&\quad + H'R^{-1}[z_{n-1} - H\hat{x}_{n-1|n}]\} \\
&= \hat{x}_{n-1|n} - \Gamma Q\Gamma'\{\Phi'H'R^{-1}[z_n - H\Phi\hat{x}_{n-1|n-1} + H\Phi\hat{x}_{n-1|n-1} - H\hat{x}_{n|n}] \\
&\quad + H'R^{-1}[z_{n-1} - H\Phi\hat{x}_{n-2|n-2} + H\Phi\hat{x}_{n-2|n-2} - H\hat{x}_{n-1|n}]\} \\
&= \hat{x}_{n-1|n} - \Gamma Q\Gamma'\{\Phi'P_{n|n}^{-1}[\hat{x}_{n|n} - \Phi\hat{x}_{n-1|n-1}] - \Phi'H'R^{-1}H[\hat{x}_{n|n} - \Phi\hat{x}_{n-1|n-1}] \\
&\quad + P_{n-1|n-1}^{-1}[\hat{x}_{n-1|n-1} - \Phi\hat{x}_{n-2|n-2}] - H'R^{-1}H[\hat{x}_{n-1|n-1} - \Phi\hat{x}_{n-2|n-2}] \\
&\quad + H'R^{-1}H[\hat{x}_{n-1|n-1} - \hat{x}_{n-1|n}]\} \\
&= \hat{x}_{n-1|n} - \Gamma Q\Gamma'\{\Phi'P_{n|n-1}^{-1}[\hat{x}_{n|n} - \Phi\hat{x}_{n-1|n-1}] \\
&\quad + P_{n-1|n-2}^{-1}[\hat{x}_{n-1|n-1} - \Phi\hat{x}_{n-2|n-2}] - H'R^{-1}H[\hat{x}_{n-1|n-1} - \hat{x}_{n-1|n}]\} \\
&= \hat{x}_{n-1|n} - \Gamma Q\Gamma'\{P_{n-1}^{-1}[\hat{x}_{n-1|n} - \hat{x}_{n-1|n-1}] \\
&\quad + P_{n-1|n-2}^{-1}[\hat{x}_{n-1|n-1} - \Phi\hat{x}_{n-2|n-2}] \\
&\quad - H'R^{-1}H[\hat{x}_{n-1|n} - \hat{x}_{n-1|n-1}]\} \\
&= \hat{x}_{n-1|n} - \Gamma Q\Gamma'\{P_{n-1|n-2}^{-1}[\hat{x}_{n-1|n} - \hat{x}_{n-1|n-1}] \\
&\quad + P_{n-1|n-2}^{-1}[\hat{x}_{n-1|n-1} - \Phi\hat{x}_{n-2|n-2}]\} \\
&= \hat{x}_{n-1|n} - \Gamma Q\Gamma'\{P_{n-1|n-2}^{-1}[\hat{x}_{n-1|n} - \Phi\hat{x}_{n-2|n-2}]\} \\
&= \Phi\hat{x}_{n-2|n-2} + [\hat{x}_{n-1|n} - \Phi\hat{x}_{n-2|n-2}] \\
&\quad - \Gamma Q\Gamma' P_{n-1|n-2}^{-1}[\hat{x}_{n-1|n} - \Phi\hat{x}_{n-2|n-2}] \\
&= \Phi\hat{x}_{n-2|n-2} + [P_{n-1|n-2} - \Gamma Q\Gamma']P_{n-1|n-2}^{-1}[\hat{x}_{n-1|n} - \Phi\hat{x}_{n-2|n-2}]
\end{aligned}
$$

Therefore,

$$\hat{x}_{n-2|n} = \hat{x}_{n-2|n-2} + \Phi^{-1}[\Phi P_{n-2|n-2}\Phi'] P_{n-1|n-2}^{-1}[\hat{x}_{n-1|n} - \Phi\hat{x}_{n-2|n-2}]$$

$$= \hat{x}_{n-2|n-2} + P_{n-2|n-2}\Phi' P_{n-1|n-2}^{-1}[\hat{x}_{n-1|n} - \Phi\hat{x}_{n-2|n-2}] \tag{3.39}$$

Extending to the general case, we have

$$\left.\begin{aligned}
\hat{x}_{i|n} &= \hat{x}_{i|i} + P_{i|i}\Phi' P_{i+1|i}^{-1}[\hat{x}_{i+1|n} - \Phi\hat{x}_{i|i}] \\
P_{i|i} &= \Phi^{-1}[P_{i+1|i} - \Gamma Q \Gamma']\Phi'^{-1} \\
P_{i|i-1}^{-1} &= P_{i|i}^{-1} - H'R^{-1}H \\
\hat{x}_{i|i} &= \Phi^{-1}\hat{x}_{i+1|i+1} - \Phi^{-1}P_{i+1|i}H'R^{-1}[z_{i+1} - H\hat{x}_{i+1|i+1}]
\end{aligned}\right\} \tag{3.40}$$

Equation 3.40 gives a set of recursive relations for the smoothing problem. Once $\hat{x}_{n|n}$ and $P_{n|n-1}$ are given, we can obtain $\hat{x}_{i|n}$ for all $i \leq n$.

3.4 The Method of the Least-Squares Fit

In this section, we look at the filtering problem from the well-known "least-squares fit" point of view. The problem of least-squares fit over finite data is treated. We derive a recursive solution for the problem by first treating the static problem using the generalized inverse, and then we shall generalize it to the dynamic case by treating it as a stepwise static problem.

3.4.1 Static Case. Consider the following algebraic relationships:

$$Ax = b \tag{3.41}$$

where A is $k \times n$ matrix, x is an unknown n-vector, and b is a known k-vector (that is, a noisy measurement vector). If $k = n$ and the determinant of A is nonzero, x could be easily solved, namely $x = A^{-1}b$. If $n \neq k$ the inverse does not exist, and we will have no unique solution. Therefore, we must aim for the best approximation in some sense. It has been shown that the best approximation is given by the so-called generalized inverse of the matrix A.[46, 47] We shall consider two typical cases here.

Case 1. A is $k \times n$, $k < n$. This is equivalent to the case in which we have fewer equations than unknowns and an infinite number of solutions exist. However, if we take the solution

$$\hat{x}^0 = A^{\#} b \tag{3.42}$$

where $A^{\#} = A'(AA')^{\#} A(A'A)^{\#} A'$ and is the generalized inverse. Then the solution $\hat{x}^0$ thus obtained is the minimum norm solution,

$$\|\hat{x}^0\|^2 \leq \|\hat{x}^1\|^2$$

where $\hat{x}^1$ = all other possible solutions. If A is maximum rank, then the solution reduces to $\hat{x}^0 = A'(AA')^{-1}b$.

Case 2. A is $k \times n$, $k > n$. Now, we have more equations than unknowns. In general, no solutions exist. However, if we consider again the generalized inverse, we will have the least-squares fit solution. In particular if A has maximum rank, we have $\hat{x} = (A'A)^{-1}A'b$. This solution could be easily derived as follows using ordinary calculus: Let

$$J = \| A\hat{x} - b \|^2$$

then

$$\frac{\partial J}{\partial \hat{x}} = 2\,[A\hat{x} - b]'A = 0$$

$$A'A\hat{x} = A'b$$

Therefore,

$$\hat{x} = (A'A)^{-1}A'b \tag{3.43}$$

Now suppose we add an additional equation to that in Case 2, say $\alpha' x = z_{k+1}$, then we have†

$$A^*_{k+1} x = b^*_{k+1}$$

where

$$A^*_{k+1} \triangleq \begin{bmatrix} A_k \\ \hline \alpha' \end{bmatrix} \qquad b^*_{k+1} \triangleq \begin{bmatrix} b_k \\ \hline z_{k+1} \end{bmatrix}$$

The solution is

†From this point on, we introduced the subscript k, k + 1 to indicate the dimension of the measurement vector b.

$$\hat{x}_{k+1} = (A^*_{k+1}{}' A^*_{k+1})^{-1} A^*_{k+1}{}' b^*_{k+1} \tag{3.44}$$

It is apparent here that to obtain the solution, we must find the inverse of the new matrix $(A^*_{k+1}{}' A^*_{k+1})$. To improve the computational efficiency, we can readily develop a recursive scheme using the matrix inversion lemma.

$$(A^*_{k+1}{}' A^*_{k+1})^{-1} = \left\{ \begin{bmatrix} A_k{}' & \vdots & \alpha \end{bmatrix} \begin{bmatrix} A_k \\ \hline \alpha' \end{bmatrix} \right\}^{-1} = [A_k{}' A_k + \alpha\alpha']^{-1}$$

Let us define

$$P_k^{-1} \triangleq A_k{}' A_k$$

$$P_{k+1}^{-1} \triangleq (A_{k+1}{}' A_{k+1}) = A_k{}' A_k + \alpha\alpha' = P_k^{-1} + \alpha\alpha'$$

then the matrix inversion lemma gives

$$P_{k+1} = P_k - P_k \alpha(\alpha' P_k \alpha + 1)^{-1} \alpha' P_k \tag{3.45}$$

Here we reduce the problem of inverting a $n \times n$ matrix to that of inverting a scalar and some multiplications and summations. This is very useful especially when n is large. Substituting Equation 3.45 into 3.44, we have the general recursive formula:

$$\begin{aligned} \hat{x}_{k+1} &= P_{k+1} [A_k{}' b_k + z_{k+1}] \\ &= P_k A_k{}' b_k + P_k z_{k+1} - P_k \alpha(\alpha' P_k \alpha + 1)^{-1} \\ &\quad \times \{\alpha' P_k [A_k{}' b_k + z_{k+1}]\} \\ &= \hat{x}_k + P_k \alpha(\alpha' P_k \alpha + 1)^{-1} (z_{k+1} - \alpha' \hat{x}_k) \end{aligned} \tag{3.46}$$

Note that the new estimate is given by the old estimate plus a linear correction term based on the new information b_{k+1}, α and the old P_k only. To start the estimation procedure using Equation 3.46, we must have $P_0, \hat{x}_0$ given. If $P_0, \hat{x}_0$ are not given, then we simply take the first set of n equations, perform the matrix inversion to obtain $P_n, \hat{x}_n$ and then uses Equation 3.46 for subsequent estimations.

It is important tu point out that this procedure is purely deterministic. We did not and need not take into consideration how the Equation 3.41 is obtained. If we further assume that Equation 3.41 comes about because of the noisy environment, then we must have the statistics of the noise if we wish to make statements concerning the quality of the estimates (that is, consistency and so forth).

Stochastic interpretation. Consider now the case where there is measurement noise contained in the vector b such that Equation 3.41 becomes

$$A_k x \triangleq \beta_k = b_k - v_k \tag{3.47}$$

where v_k is a white Gaussian random vector with zero mean and covariance

$$R = \sigma^2 I$$

β_k is the true measurement vector and b_k is the actual noisy measurement vector. Since we cannot measure v_k, we will proceed by assuming

$$A_k x = b_k$$

and proceed to solve it as shown in Equation 3.43. The question now is whether the solution is statistically consistent or not. We proceed as follows: From Equation 3.43, we have

$$\hat{x}_k = (A_k' A_k)^{-1} A_k' b_k$$

where k = dimension of the measurement vector. Premultiplying Equation 3.47 by $(A_k' A_k)^{-1} A_k'$, we have

$$(A_k' A_k)^{-1} A_k' A_k x = (A_k' A_k)^{-1} A_k' b_k - (A_k' A_k)^{-1} A_k' v_k$$

Therefore,

$$x = \hat{x}_k - (A_k' A_k)^{-1} A_k' v_k$$

hence,

$$\tilde{x}_k \triangleq \hat{x}_k - x = (A_k' A_k)^{-1} A_k' v_k$$

Averaging, and, assuming the independence of A_k and v_k, we have

$$\overline{\tilde{x}_k} = \overline{(A_k{}'A_k)^{-1}A_k'v_k}$$

$$= \overline{(A_k{}'A_k)^{-1}A_k{}'}\,\bar{v}_k = 0$$

Hence the estimate $\hat{x}_k$ is unbiased. The covariance matrix

$$\tilde{P}_k \triangleq \overline{\tilde{x}_k\tilde{x}_k{}'} = \overline{(A_k{}'A_k)^{-1}A_k{}'v_kv_k{}'A_k(A_k{}'A_k)^{-1}}$$

$$= (A_k{}'A_k)^{-1}A_k{}'RA_k(A_k{}'A_k)^{-1}$$

$$= \sigma^2(A_k{}'A_k)^{-1}$$

$$\equiv \sigma^2 P_k$$

where

$$P_k \triangleq (A_k{}'A_k)^{-1}$$

Hence, we can rewrite Equations 3.46 and 3.45 as follows:

$$\hat{x}_{k+1} = \hat{x}_k + \tilde{P}_k\alpha(\alpha'\tilde{P}_k\alpha + \sigma^2)^{-1}(z_{k+1} - \alpha'\hat{x}_k)$$

$$\tilde{P}_{k+1} = \tilde{P}_k - \tilde{P}_k\alpha(\alpha'\tilde{P}_k\alpha + \sigma^2)^{-1}\alpha'\tilde{P}_k$$

Note that the covariance matrix $\tilde{P}_k$ always decreases and in the limit $\rightarrow [0]$ as $k \rightarrow \infty$. Hence, we can conclude that the estimate is statistically consistent.

3.4.2 Dynamic Case. Now let us give a dynamic interpretation[9, 20, 21] to the solution we obtained in Case 1. Consider that the x, z are given by a dynamic relationship,

$$\left.\begin{aligned} x_{k+1} &= \Phi x_k \\ z_k &= h'x_k + v_k \end{aligned}\right\} \tag{3.49}$$

where Φ and h may be time varying and where v_k are white noise with zero mean and variance σ^2. We are interested in estimating x_{k+1}, given $z_1, z_2, \ldots, z_{k+1}$.

Solution. Proceeding as before, we have the equations

$$\begin{bmatrix} A_k \Phi^{-1} \\ \hline h' \end{bmatrix} \begin{bmatrix} x_{k+1} \end{bmatrix} = \begin{bmatrix} z_1 \\ \vdots \\ z_k \\ \hline z_{k+1} \end{bmatrix} = \begin{bmatrix} b_k \\ \hline z_{k+1} \end{bmatrix}$$

where

$$A_k \triangleq \begin{bmatrix} h'\Phi^{-k+1} \\ \vdots \\ h'\Phi^{-1} \\ h' \end{bmatrix}$$

Again let us define

$$P_k \triangleq (A_k{}'A_k)^{-1}$$

$$P_{k+1} \triangleq (\Phi^{-1\prime} A_k{}' A_k \Phi^{-1} + hh')^{-1}$$

$$\triangleq (M_{k+1}{}^{-1} + hh')^{-1}$$

Applying the matrix inversion lemma, we have

$$\left.\begin{aligned} P_{k+1} &= M_{k+1} - M_{k+1} h(h'M_{k+1} h + 1)^{-1} h'M_{k+1} \\ M_{k+1} &= \Phi P_k \Phi' \end{aligned}\right\} \qquad (3.50)$$

Proceeding analogous to Equations 3.45 and 3.46, we have

$$\hat{x}_{k+1|k+1} = P_{k+1}[A_k{}' b_k + hz_{k+1}]$$

$$= \Phi\hat{x}_{k|k} + M_{k+1}h(h'M_{k+1}h + 1)^{-1}[z_{k+1} - h'\Phi\hat{x}_{k|k}] \qquad (3.51)$$

Note that we have introduced a new set of subscripts $(k|k)$ here, and $\hat{x}_{k|k}$ implies the estimate of x at time k given measurements up to and including z_k. Giving a stochastic interpretation to Equation 3.51 similar to that shown in Section 3.4.1, we have

$$P_k = \frac{\tilde{P}_{k|k}}{\sigma^2}$$

$$M_{k+1} = \Phi P_k \Phi' = \frac{1}{\sigma^2} \Phi \tilde{P}_k \Phi'$$

$$\equiv \frac{1}{\sigma^2} \tilde{P}_{k+1|k}$$

where $\tilde{P}_{k|k}$ is the covariance matrix of $x_{k|k}$ and $\tilde{P}_{k+1|k}$ is the extrapolated covariance matrix. Hence, our solution becomes

$$\hat{x}_{k+1|k+1} = \Phi\hat{x}_{k|k} + \tilde{P}_{k+1|k} h(h'\tilde{P}_{k+1|k} h + \sigma^2)^{-1}(z_{k+1} - h'\Phi\hat{x}_{k|k})$$

$$\tilde{P}_{k+1|k} = \Phi\tilde{P}_{k|k}\Phi' \tag{3.52}$$

$$\tilde{P}_{k+1|k+1} = \tilde{P}_{k+1|k} - \tilde{P}_{k+1|k} h(h'\tilde{P}_{k+1|k} h + \sigma^2)^{-1} h'\tilde{P}_{k+1|k}$$

To go one step further, let us assume that we have actually the relationship

$$\left.\begin{aligned} x_{k+1} &= \Phi x_k + \Gamma w_k \\ z_k &= H x_k + v_k \end{aligned}\right\} \tag{3.53}$$

where z_k, v_k, w_k are vectors, Γ, Φ, H are known, and w, v are white Gaussian noise vector sequences;

$$E(w_k) = E(v_k) = 0$$

$$E(v_k v_j') = R\delta_{kj}$$

$$E(w_k w_j') = Q\delta_{kj}$$

$$E(v_k, w_j') = 0$$

The solution becomes

$$\hat{x}_{k+1|k+1} = \Phi\hat{x}_{k|k} + \tilde{P}_{k+1|k} H'(H\tilde{P}_{k+1|k} H' + R)^{-1}(z_{k+1} - H\Phi\hat{x}_{k|k})$$

$$\tilde{P}_{k+1|k+1} = \tilde{P}_{k+1|k} - \tilde{P}_{k+1|k} H'(H\tilde{P}_{k+1|k} H' + R)^{-1} H\tilde{P}_{k+1|k} \tag{3.54}$$

$$\tilde{P}_{k+1|k} = \Phi\tilde{P}_{k|k}\Phi' + \Gamma Q \Gamma'$$

These are again precisely the Wiener-Kalman estimation formulas. Note that $\tilde{P}_{k+1|k}$ is now the extrapolated covariance matrix obtained from Equation 3.53 and the property of the Gaussian noise.

3.5 The Method of Maximum-Likelihood Estimation

The method of maximum likelihood is an old standard technique developed by Fisher to be used in point estimation of parameters. The basic concept is quite simple and can be found in most standard texts in probability and statistics. As the name implies, the fundamental idea is to define a so-called likelihood function, usually the conditional probability $p(z|x)$ relating the parameter x and the sample measurements z. Then this likelihood function is maximized with respect to the parameters. To illustrate the basic concept better, consider the parameter estimation problem as follows:

Problem: Assume that we know the form of the probability density function of y, say $p(y) = p(y, x)$, where x is some unknown parameter. Now take a few independent measurements say $y_1, y_2, \cdots, y_n$. Question: What is the best estimate of x based on these measurements?

Solution: To find the solution to this problem, we ask ourselves this equestion. "What parameters x will make this set of measurements $z' = (y_1, y_2, \cdots, y_n)$ most likely to occur? To do this we proceed as follows:

1. Set up a likelihood function

$$L(z, x) = p(z|x)$$

2. Find the parameter x which maximizes this likelihood function. Hence the solution must satisfy the condition $\partial L/\partial x = 0$, $\partial^2 L/\partial x^2 < 0$. Hence this statistical estimation problem is reduced to that of finding the likelihood function and then the simple application of ordinary calculus. Armed with this basic concept of the maximum-likelihood estimate, we proceed to the state estimation problem.

First we will consider the static case (single stage).

Problem: Consider the vector equation

$$z = Ax + v \tag{3.55}$$

where z is the measurement vector $(\gamma \times 1)$, x is the unknown constant (state) vector (static) $(n \times 1)$, v is random noise $(\gamma \times 1)$ independent of x, and A is a $\gamma \times n$ rectangular matrix $(\gamma \geq n)$. Question: Given the statistics of v, for what value of x will z most likely occur?

Solution: Find x that maximizes the conditional probability $p(z|x)\,dz$. Let

$$
\begin{aligned}
L(x) &= p(z|x) \\
&= \frac{p(z, x)}{p(x)} = \frac{p(x, v)\dagger}{p(x)} \\
&= \frac{p(x)p(v)}{p(x)} \\
&= p(v) \triangleq p_v(z - Ax)\ddagger
\end{aligned}
\tag{3.56}
$$

To find the best estimates of x in the maximum-likelihood sense, we simply set

$$
\frac{\partial L}{\partial x} = \frac{\partial p_v(z - Ax)}{\partial x} = 0
$$

Now, assuming that the noise v is white Gaussian with zero mean and covariance matrix I, then we have

$$
\begin{aligned}
L(x) = p(v) &= \frac{1}{2\pi^{\frac{\gamma}{2}} |I|^{\frac{1}{2}}} \exp\left[-\frac{1}{2} v' I^{-1} v\right] \\
&= c \exp\left[-\frac{1}{2} (z - Ax)' I^{-1} (z - Ax)\right] \\
&= c \exp\left[-\frac{1}{2} ||z - Ax||^2\right]
\end{aligned}
\tag{3.57}
$$

To maximize L(x), we must minimize the exponent $||z - Ax||^2$, hence the problem is identical to the simple least-squares fit problem discussed earlier and the results will be and must be the same as that given in Equation 3.48. As was shown in Section 3.4, if the dimension of z is increased by one at a time, we can readily derive a recursive relationship (Equation 3.48) to update our estimates.

Now let us consider the dynamic case (multistage).

Problem: Now consider the case where the state vectors x_i are the output of linear dynamic system and are themselves random sequences as shown in Figure 3.6, where

---

†The Jacobian J is an identity matrix in this case.

‡$p_v(z - Ax)$ implies the substitution of $(z - Ax) = v$ into $p(v)$.

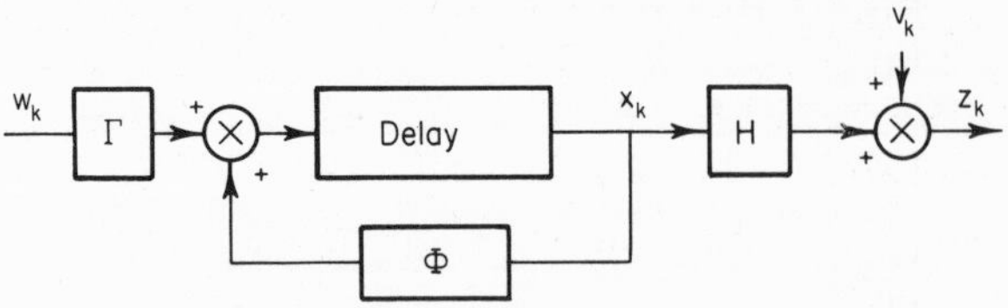

Figure 3.6. Model of the dynamic system.

$$\left.\begin{aligned} x_{k+1} &= \Phi x_k + \Gamma w_k \\ z_k &= H x_k + v_k \end{aligned}\right\} \tag{3.58}$$

Now the question becomes: Given the statistics of w, v the matrixes Φ, H, Γ, and the measurements $z_0, z_1, \cdots, z_m$, what are the sequences $x_0, x_1, \cdots, x_m$ that will make the z's most likely to happen?

Solution: Define

$$\begin{aligned} L(x_0, x_1, x_2, \cdots, x_m) &= p(z_0, z_1, \cdots, z_m | x_0, x_1, \cdots, x_m) \\ &= \frac{p(z_0, z_1, \cdots, z_m, x_0, x_1, \cdots, x_m)}{p(x_0, x_1, x_2, \cdots, x_m)} \\ &= \frac{p(v_0, v_1, v_2, \cdots, v_m, x_0, x_1, \cdots, x_m)}{p(x_0, x_1, \cdots, x_m)} \\ &= p(v_0, v_1, v_2, \cdots, v_m) \end{aligned} \tag{3.59}$$

if the v's are independent of the x's.

Therefore, the maximum-likelihood solution becomes the problem of finding the sequence $x_0, x_1, \cdots, x_m$ which maximizes $L(x_0, x_1, \cdots, x_m)$ subject to the constraint $x_{k+1} = \Phi x_k + \Gamma w_k$ where $k = 0, \cdots, m - 1$. Again, in the Gaussian case, this problem simply reduces to

$$\min \sum_{i=1}^{m} \|z_i - Hx_i\|^2_{R^{-1}}$$

subject to the constraint $x_{i+1} = \Phi x_i + \Gamma w_i$, where $i = 0, \cdots, m - 1$. The solution to this problem is analogous to that of the least-squares fit with a dynamic interpretation. (See Section 3.4.2.) The results are, from Equation 3.54,

$$\hat{x}_{k+1|k+1} = \Phi\hat{x}_{k|k} + \tilde{P}_{k+1|k}H'(H\tilde{P}_{k+1|k}H' + R)^{-1}(z_{k+1} - H\Phi\hat{x}_{k|k})$$

$$\tilde{P}_{k+1|k} = \Phi\tilde{P}_{k|k}\Phi' + \Gamma Q\Gamma' \tag{3.60}$$

$$\tilde{P}_{k+1} = \tilde{P}_{k+1|k} - \tilde{P}_{k+1|k}H'(H\tilde{P}_{k+1|k}H' + R)^{-1}H\tilde{P}_{k+1|k}$$

where the $\tilde{P}$'s are covariance matrices.

If the a priori information $\tilde{P}_{0|0}$ and $\hat{x}_{0|0}$ are given, the above results are identical to that of the Kalman filter given in Section 3.2. If this information is not given, then we must take the first set of n-equations, solve for $\tilde{P}_n, x_n$ by direct matrix inversion. From n + 1 on, Equation 3.60 will provide the subsequent solutions.

3.6 The Bayesian Approach to the Stochastic Estimation Problem†

Now, let us look at this problem of stochastic estimation from a more general point of view. Consider now that the states x and the measurements z are somehow related (linear, nonlinear, and so forth), and the problem is, "Given the measurements z, what is the best estimate of x (in some sense)?" To solve this problem, the best thing to do is to determine the a posteriori conditional density function $p(x|z)$, since it contains all the statistical information of interest. This is the key to the Bayesian approach. See Figure 3.7. Knowing the density function $p(x|z)$, we can readily

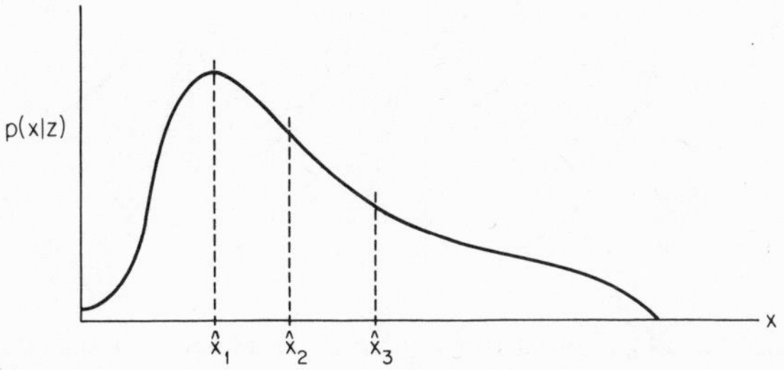

Figure 3.7. Conditional probability density function.

determine the various estimates x_1, x_2, x_3, and so forth, which are optimal in some sense. Three of these possible estimates are as follows:

†The materials contained in Sections 3.6 and 3.7 are the results of a joint effort[23] of the author and Professor Y. C. Ho of Harvard University.

1. The most probable† estimate is $\hat{x}_1$, the x that is most likely to happen; this is the mode of the density function.
2. The conditional mean is $\hat{x}_2$, the solution to

$$\min \int_{-\infty}^{\infty} ||x - \hat{x}||^2 \, p(x|z) \, dx$$

   Note that this is the so-called equal risk estimate where the probability of x being larger or smaller than $\hat{x}_2$ is the same.
3. The minimax estimate is $\hat{x}_3$, the estimate that minimizes the maximum possible error $|x - \hat{x}_3|$. This is simply the median.

Depending upon the requirements at hand, we then define the best estimate. It is noteworthy to point out here that if $p(x|z)$ is Gaussian, then $\hat{x}_1, \hat{x}_2, \hat{x}_3$ are all the same. (This is obvious from the shape of the Gaussian distribution; in fact, this is true in general for all single-mode symmetrical functions.) Knowing $p(x|z's)$, we obtain the additional knowledge concerning the confidence interval, bias, consistency, and so forth of the estimates. In the multistage estimation problem, the knowledge $p(x_i|z_i)$ for all i offers considerable intuitive feel to the engineer, since it converts a stochastic problem into a series of deterministic pictures or relationships which he can visualize and manipulate. For example, if $p(x|z_i)$ are of the forms (scalar case) of Figure 3.8,

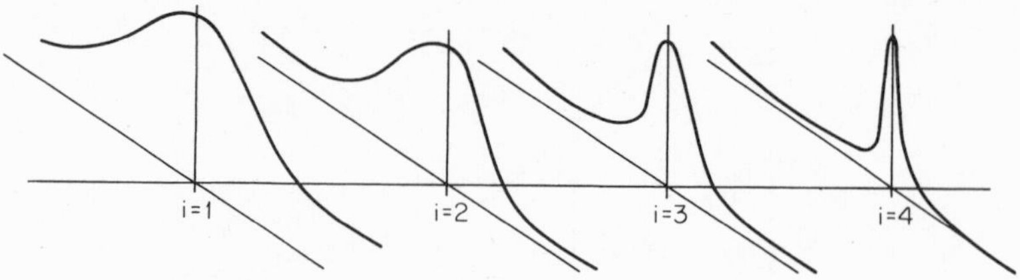

Figure 3.8. Case 1: Transitions of conditional probability density functions.

he can readily determine what the estimate should be and how good it is. On the other hand, if they are of the forms of Figure 3.9, he will conclude that perhaps he is not measuring the right things. In many instances, the Bayesian approach offers considerable advantage also if we wish to derive recursive relationships relating the current and past estimates. This will be dis-

†The maximum-likelihood estimate in the Bayesian sense. We use a different name here to distinguish it from that of the classical maximum-likelihood estimate (Section 3.5).

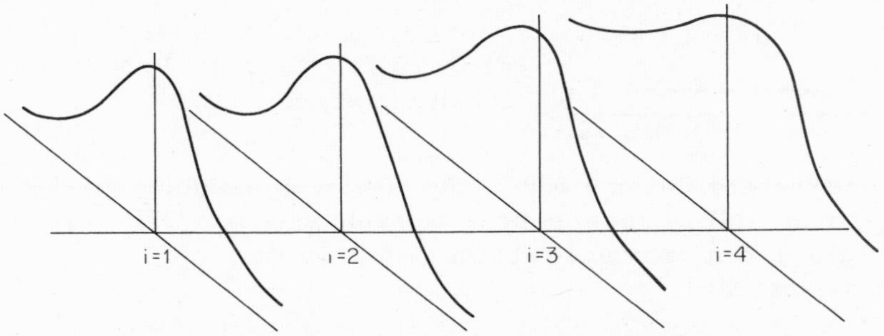

Figure 3.9. Case 2: Transitions of conditional probability density functions.

cussed in detail later. In general, the conditional density function $p(x|z)$ can be evaluated as follows:

$$p(x|z) = \frac{p(x, z)}{p(z)}$$

$$= \frac{p(z|x)p(x)}{p(z)} \quad \text{(Bayes rule)} \tag{3.61}$$

where $p(x)$ is the a priori density function of x, and $p(z)$ is the density function of the measurements. Therefore one can obtain $p(x|z)$ if (a) the joint density $p(x, z)$ is given or can be calculated based on the information given, or (b) if the conditional density function $p(z|x)$ is given or can be readily computed. Dependent on the nature of the problem, we may prefer step a or b.

From Equation 3.61, it is obvious that a priori information on x is necessary in order to obtain the density function $p(x|z)$. In general, this information is obtained as follows:

Case 1. No a priori information available: In this case, assume that all x's are equally likely, hence $p(x) = \lim_{a\to\infty} \frac{1}{2a}$. See Figure 3.10.

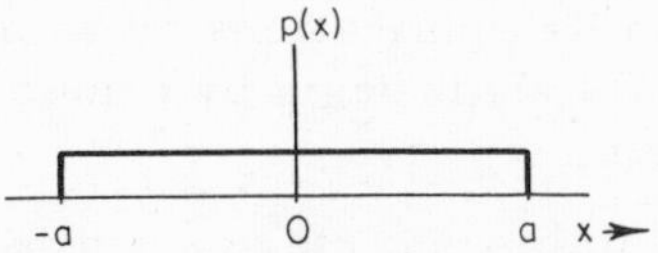

Figure 3.10. Case 1: Probability density function of x.

Case 2. No a priori information given other than the bounds due to physical or other limits: Here we assume that x is constrained to be within -b and +a. Without further information, one simply assumes that all x's are equally likely within this range, hence $p(x) = \frac{1}{a + b}$. See Figure 3.11.

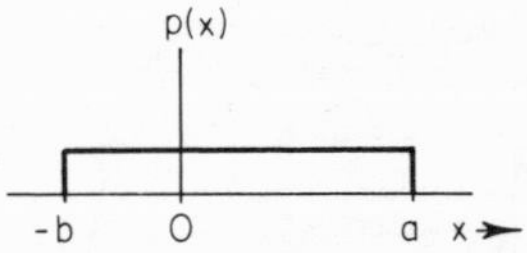

Figure 3.11. Case 2: Probability density function of x.

Note that for Cases 1 and 2, the classical maximum-likelihood estimate (MLE) and the most probable estimate (MPE) are identical. It can be readily shown as follows:
Classical MLE,

$$\frac{\partial p(z|x)}{\partial x} = 0$$

Bayesian MPE,

$$\frac{\partial p(x|z)}{\partial x} = 0$$

But

$$\frac{\partial p(x|z)}{\partial x} = \frac{\partial}{\partial x} \left[\frac{p(z|x)p(x)}{p(z)}\right]$$

$$= \text{const} \frac{\partial}{\partial x} p(z|x)$$

since p(x) and p(z) are not functions of x. Therefore, we would expect the solutions to be the same as long as it falls within the acceptable bounds shown in Case 2.

Case 3. A priori knowledge due to prior measurements: In a multistage estimation problem, we would like to obtain the optimal estimate based on the latest information. If we have $p(x_i|z_i)$ based on i-th prior measurements, this density function or some function of it will provide sufficient a priori information for us to proceed to the (i + 1)-th stage.

Having discussed the basic concepts of the Bayesian approach, we shall illustrate its applications by using it to solve some specific problems. We shall begin by considering the single-stage estimation problem.

Problem: The following information is assume given:

1. The physical relationships are

$$z = g(x, v)$$

where z is the measurement vector ($\gamma \times 1$), x is the state (signal) vector ($n \times 1$), and v is the noise vector ($q \times 1$).

2. The joint density function p(x, v); from this we can readily obtain the respective marginals, p(x) and p(v). We assume

information for Item 2 is available in analytical form or can be approximated by analytical distributions. Item 1 can be either in close form or merely computable. We are required to obtain an estimate $\hat{x}$ of x which is best, in some sense to be defined later.

The Bayesian Solution: The Bayesian solution to the single-stage estimation problem now proceeds via the following steps:

1. Evaluate p(z). This can be done analytically, at least in principle, or experimentally by the Monte Carlo method since z = g(x, v) and p(x, v) are given. In the latter case, we assume it is possible to fit the experimental distribution again by a member of a family of distributions.

2. At this point, two alternatives are possible; one may be superior to the other dependent on the nature of the problem.

a. Evaluate p(x,z). This is possible analytically if v is of the same dimension as z and we can obtain the functional relationship v = h(x,z) from the physical relationship given. In this case from the theory of derived distributions, we have

$$p(x,z) = p[x, h(x, z)]\,J$$

where

$$J = \det\left[\frac{\partial h(x, z)}{\partial z}\right]$$

b. Evaluate p(z| x). This conditional density function can always be obtained either analytically, whenever possible, or experimentally, from the z = g(x, v) and p(x, v).

Note that step 2a may be difficult to obtain in general since h may not exist, either because of the nonlinear nature or because z, v are of different dimensions. Nevertheless, step 2b can always be carried out. This fact will be demonstrated in the nonlinear example in the following.

3. Evaluate p(x|z) using the following relationship:

a. Following step 2a, we have

$$p(x|z) = \frac{p(x, z)}{p(z)} \tag{3.62}$$

b. Following step 2b and using the Bayes theorem, we have

$$p(x|z) = \frac{p(z|x)p(x)}{p(z)} \tag{3.63}$$

The class of distribution we have assumed or obtained for p(x, v), p(z) determines how easy or difficult this key step may be to carry out. Several classes of distribution that have nice properties for this purpose can be found in Reference 49, pp. 53 to 58. The density function $p(x|z)$ is known as the a posteriori density function of x. It is our state of knowledge of nature after the measurements z. By definition, it contains all the information necessary for estimation.

4. Depending on the criterion function for estimation, we can compute estimate $\hat{x}$ from $p(x|z)$.

Special Case of the Wiener-Kalman Filter (single stage): Now let us consider a special case of the single-stage estimation problem. Let $p(x)$ be Gaussian with

$$\left.\begin{aligned} E(x) &= \bar{x} \\ \operatorname{cov}(x) &= P_0 \end{aligned}\right\} \tag{3.64}$$

Let $p(v)$ be Gaussian with

$$\left.\begin{aligned} E(v) &= 0 \\ \operatorname{cov}(v) &= R \end{aligned}\right\} \tag{3.65}$$

$$z = Hx + v \text{ (physical relationship)} \tag{3.66}$$

$$p(x, v) = p(x)p(v) \tag{3.67}$$

Now following the steps for the Bayesian solution, we have

1. Evaluate $p(z)$. Since $z = Hx + v$ and x, v are Gaussian and independent, we immediately get since $p(z)$ is Gaussian

$$\left.\begin{aligned} E(z) &= H\bar{x} \\ \operatorname{cov}(z) &= HP_0H' + R \end{aligned}\right\} \tag{3.68}$$

2a. Evaluating $p(z, x)$, we have

$$\frac{\partial h}{\partial z} = \text{identity matrix}$$

Thus

$$\begin{aligned} p(x, z) &= p(x, v) = p(x)p(v) \\ &= p(x)p_v(z - Hx) \end{aligned} \tag{3.69}$$

2b. Evaluating $p(z|x)$, we have†

†Note: This step is redundant.

$$p(z|x) = \frac{p(x, z)}{p(x)} = p(v) = p_v(z - Hx) \tag{3.70}$$

where $p_v(z - Hx)$ implies that we substitute $v = z - Hx$ into $p(v)$.

3. Evaluating $p(x|z)$, we have,

$$p(x|z) = \frac{p(x)p(v)}{p(z)} \tag{3.71}$$

By direct substitution of Equations 3.64, 3.65, and 3.68, we get, after some manipulation,

$$\begin{aligned} p(x|z) = \text{const} \exp \Big\{ -\frac{1}{2} [(x - \bar{x})'(P_0^{-1}) (x - \bar{x}) \\ + (z - Hx)' R^{-1} (z - Hx) \\ - (z - H\bar{x})'(HP_0H' + R)^{-1}(z - H\bar{x})] \Big\} \end{aligned} \tag{3.72}$$

Now completing squares in the braces, we get

$$p(x|z) = \text{const} \exp \Big\{ -\frac{1}{2} [(x - \hat{x})' P^{-1}(x - \hat{x})] \Big\} \tag{3.73}$$

where

$$P^{-1} = P_0^{-1} + H'R^{-1}H$$

or, equivalently,

$$P = P_0 - P_0H'(HP_0H' + R)^{-1}HP_0 \tag{3.74}$$

and

$$\hat{x} = \bar{x} + PH'R^{-1}(z - H\bar{x}) \tag{3.75}$$

4. Now since $p(x|z)$ is Gaussian, the most probable estimate, the conditional mean, and minimax estimate all coincide and are given by $\hat{x}$. This is the derivation of the single-stage Wiener-Kalman filter.[30, 31] The P, x pair is called a sufficient statistic for the problem in the sense that $p(x|z) = p(x|P, \hat{x})$.

Having thus solved the single-stage estimation problem, we now proceed in similar manner to the general multistage estimation problem.

Problem: It is assumed that at any time (stage) $k + 1$ we are given, as a result of previous calculation and as part of the problem statement, the following data:

1. A priori density function,† $p(x_k | z_k, z_{k-1}, \cdots, z_1) \triangleq p(x_k | Z_k)$.
2. Statistics $p(w_k, v_{k+1} | x_k, Z_k)$ of a vector random sequence with vector components w_k and v_{k+1} which depend on x_k and $z_k, \cdots, z_1$.‡
3.

$$x_{k+1} = f(x_k, w_k)$$

$$z_k = h(x_k, v_k)$$

$$= h(f(x_{k-1}, w_{k-1}), v_k)$$

$$= g(x_{k-1}, w_{k-1}, v_k)$$

which is the physical model of the Markov random sequence x and its relationship to z.

Now an extra set of measurements z_{k+1} is made and we are asked to estimate x_{k+1} based on $z_{k+1} \ldots z_1$.

Solution: In analogous manner to the single-stage case, the solution is given in four steps:

1a. Evaluate $p(x_{k+1}, v_{k+1} | Z_k)$. This is accomplished analytically or experimentally by knowing $x_{k+1} = f(x_k, w_k)$, and $p(x_k | z_k)$, and $p(w_k, v_{k+1} | x_k, Z_k)$.

1b. Evaluate $p(z_{k+1} | Z_k)$. This is obtained via step 1a and $z_{k+1} = h(x_{k+1}, v_{k+1})$.

2a. Evaluate $p(x_{k+1}, z_{k+1} | Z_k)$. As before we have

$$p(x_{k+1}, z_{k+1} | Z_k) = p(x_{k+1}, V_{k+1} | Z_k) J \tag{3.76}$$

where

$$J = \det\left(\frac{\partial g}{\partial z_{k+1}}\right) \qquad v_{k+1} \triangleq g(x_{k+1}, z_{k+1}) \tag{3.77}$$

2b. Evaluate $p(z_{k+1} | x_{k+1}, Z_k)$. This is given by

$$p(z_{k+1} | x_{k+1}, Z_k) = \frac{p(z_{k+1}, x_{k+1} | Z_k)}{p(x_{k+1} | Z_k)} \tag{3.78}$$

or experimentally from the problem statement.

---

†We have adopted the simplifying notation $p(\cdot | Z_k)$, to mean $p(\cdot | z_k, \cdots, z_1)$.

‡Steps 1 and 2 yield $p(x_k, w_k, v_{k+1} | Z_k)$. We also assume that if $p(w_k, v_{k+1} | x_k, Z_k) = p(w_k, v_{k+1})$ then (w_k, v_{k+1}) is a white (completely) random sequence.

3. Evaluate, analytically, $p(x_{k+1}|Z_{k+1})$ using result from steps 2a or 2b,

$$p(x_{k+1}|Z_{k+1}) = \frac{p(z_{k+1}|x_{k+1}, Z_k)\, p(x_{k+1}|Z_k)}{p(z_{k+1}|Z_k)}$$

$$= \frac{p(x_{k+1}, v_{k+1}|Z_k)\, J}{p(z_{k+1}|Z_k)} \tag{3.79}$$

At this point, steps 1 and 3 can be repeated to obtain $p(x_t|Z_t)$ for all t.

4. Estimates for x_{k+1} can be calculated from $p(x_{k+1}|Z_{k+1})$ similarly as in the single-stage case.

Special Case of the Wiener-Kalman Filter: The given data at k + 1 are specificed as follows:

$p(x_k|Z_k)$:

$$\left.\begin{aligned} E(x_k|Z_k) &= \hat{x}_{k|k} \\ \text{cov}\,(x_k|Z_k) &= P_{k|k} \end{aligned}\right\} \tag{3.80}$$

$p(w_k, v_{k+1}|x_k, Z_k) = p(w_k, v_{k+1}) = p(w_k)p(v_{k+1})$:

$$\left.\begin{aligned} &E(v_k) = E(v_{k+1}) = 0 \\ &\text{cov}\,(w_k) = Q \qquad \text{cov}\,(v_k) = R \end{aligned}\right\} \tag{3.81}$$

that is, w and v are independent, white, Gaussian and random sequences, and the physical relationship is

$$\left.\begin{aligned} x_{k+1} &= \Phi x_k + \Gamma w_k \\ z_k &= H x_k + v_k \end{aligned}\right\} \tag{3.82}$$

where H maybe time varying. The steps leading to the solution can now be given:

1a and 1b. Evaluate $p(x_{k+1}, v_{k+1}|Z_k)$, $p(z_{k+1}|Z_k)$. From Equation 3.82, we note that $p(x_{k+1}|Z_k)$ is Gaussian and independent of v_{k+1}, with

$$\left.\begin{aligned} E(x_{k+1}|Z_k) &= \Phi\hat{x}_{k|k} \\ \operatorname{cov}(x_{k+1}|Z_k) &= \Phi P_{k|k}\Phi' + \Gamma Q \Gamma' \triangleq P_{k+1|k} \end{aligned}\right\} \tag{3.83}$$

Similarly, $p(Z_{k+1}|Z_k)$ is Gaussian and

$$\left.\begin{aligned} E(z_{k+1}|Z_k) &= H\Phi\hat{x}_{k|k} \\ \operatorname{cov}(z_{k+1}|Z_k) &= HP_{k+1|k}H' + R \end{aligned}\right\} \tag{3.84}$$

2a. Evaluate $P(x_{k+1}, z_{k+1}|Z_k)$. Again, as in the single-stage case, we have

$$\det\left(\frac{\partial g}{\partial z_{k+1}}\right) = J = 1$$

Therefore,

$$\begin{aligned} p(x_{k+1}, z_{k+1}|Z_k) &= p(x_{k+1}, v_{k+1}|Z_k) \\ &= p(x_{k+1}|Z_k)\, p(v_{k+1}) \\ &= p(x_{k+1}|Z_k)\, p(z_{k+1} - Hx_{k+1}) \end{aligned} \tag{3.85}$$

2b. Evaluate $p(z_{k+1}|x_{k+1}, Z_k)$.† From Equation 3.85, we get, directly,

$$p(z_{k+1}|x_{k+1}, Z_k) = p(v_{k+1}) = p_v(z_{k+1} - Hx_{k+1}) \tag{3.86}$$

3. Evaluate $p(x_{k+1}|Z_{k+1})$. We have

$$p(x_{k+1}|Z_{k+1}) = \frac{p_v(z_{k+1} - Hx_{k+1})\, p(x_{k+1}|Z_k)}{p(z_{k+1}|Z_k)}$$

$$\begin{aligned} = \text{const} \exp \Big\{ -\tfrac{1}{2}\big[&(x_{k+1} - \Phi\hat{x}_{k|k})' P_{k+1|k}^{-1} (x_{k+1} - \Phi\hat{x}_{k|k}) \\ &+ (z_{k+1} - Hx_{k+1})' R^{-1} (z_{k+1} - Hx_{k+1}) \\ &- (z_{k+1} - H\Phi\hat{x}_{k|k})' (HP_{k+1|k}H' + R)^{-1} (z_{k+1} - H\Phi\hat{x}_{k|k}) \big] \Big\} \end{aligned} \tag{3.87}$$

† 2b is again redundant as in the single-stage case.

Now completing squares in the brace, we get

$$p(x_{k+1}|Z_{k+1}) = \text{const}\ \exp\left\{-\frac{1}{2}[(x_{k+1} - \hat{x}_{k+1|k+1})' P_{k+1|k+1}^{-1}(x_{k+1} - \hat{x}_{k+1|k+1})]\right\} \tag{3.88}$$

where

$$\hat{x}_{k+1|k+1} = \Phi\hat{x}_{k|k} + P_{k+1|k}H'(HP_{k+1|k}H' + R)^{-1}(z_{k+1} - H\Phi\hat{x}_{k|k})$$

$$P_{k+1|k+1}^{-1} = P_{k+1|k}^{-1} + H'R^{-1}H \tag{3.89}$$

or, equivalently,

$$P_{k+1|k+1} = P_{k+1|k} - P_{k+1|k}H'(HP_{k+1|k}H' + R)^{-1}HP_{k+1|k} \tag{3.90}$$

and

$$P_{k+1|k} = \Phi P_{k|k}\Phi' + \Gamma Q\Gamma' \tag{3.91}$$

Equations 3.89 to 3.91 are exactly the discrete Wiener-Kalman filter in the multistage case.[26, 30, 31]

Having solved the multistage filtering problem, let us proceed to the multistage smoothing problem.

Problem: It is assumed that the following data are available:

1. $p(x_k|Z_k)$
2. $p(w_k, v_{k+1}|x_k, Z_k)$
3. The dynamic relationship

$$x_{k+1} = f(x_k, w_k)$$

$$z_k = h(x_k, v_k)$$

$$= g(x_{k-1}, w_{k-1}, v_k)$$

(Note that the data 1, 2, and 3 are quite similar to that of the filtering problem.) Now given a new measurement z_{k+1}, what is the best estimate of x_k based on all these measurements $z_1, z_2, \cdots, z_k, z_{k+1}$?

The Bayesian Solution: Analogous to the filtering problem, the key to the solution of the smoothing problem is to obtain the density function $p(x_k|Z_{k+\gamma})$ where $\gamma > 0$. We proceed as follows:

1. General expression: (increasing measurement data)

$$p(x_k|Z_{k+\gamma}) = p(x_k|z_{k+\gamma}, z_{k+\gamma-1}, \cdots, z_{k+1}, Z_k)$$

$$= \frac{p(z_{k+\gamma}, z_{k+\gamma-1}, \cdots, z_{k+1}, x_k|Z_k))}{p(z_{k+\gamma}, \cdots, z_{k+1}|Z_k)}$$

$$= \frac{p(z_{k+\gamma}, \cdots, z_{k+1}|x_k, Z_k)\, p(x_k|Z_k)}{p(z_{k+\gamma}, \cdots, z_{k+1}|Z_k)}$$

$$= \frac{p(Z_{k+\gamma}|x_k, Z_{k+\gamma-1})}{p(z_{k+\gamma}|Z_{k+\gamma-1})\, p(z_{k+\gamma-1}|Z_{k+\gamma-2})}$$

$$\cdots \frac{p(z_{k+1}|x_k, Z_k)\, p(x_k|Z_k)}{p(z_{k+1}|Z_k)}$$

$$\equiv \frac{p(z_{k+\gamma}|Z_{k+\gamma-1}, x_k)}{p(z_{k+\gamma}|Z_{k+\gamma-1})} \quad p(x_k|Z_{k+\gamma-1}) \tag{3.92}$$

2. General expression: (finite measurement)

$$p(x_{n-i}|Z_n) = p(x_{n-i}|z_n, z_{n-1}, \cdots, Z_{n-i})$$

$$= \frac{p(x_{n-i}, z_n, z_{n-1}, \cdots, z_{n-i+1}|Z_{n-i})}{p(z_n, z_{n-1}, \cdots, z_{n-i+1}|Z_{n-i})}$$

$$= \frac{p(z_n, z_{n-1}, \cdots, z_{n-i+1}|Z_{n-i}, x_{n-i})\, p(x_{n-i}|Z_{n-i})}{p(z_n, z_{n-1}, \cdots, z_{n-i+1}|Z_{n-i})}$$

$$= \frac{p(z_n|x_{n-i}, Z_{n-1})\, p(z_{n-1}|x_{n-i}, Z_{n-2})}{p(z_n|Z_{n-1})\, p(z_{n-1}|Z_{n-2})}$$

$$\cdots \frac{p(z_{n-i+1}|x_{n-i}, Z_{n-i})\, p(x_{n-i}|Z_{n-i})}{p(z_{n-i+1}|Z_{n-i})} \tag{3.93}$$

Once $p(x_k|Z_{k+\gamma})$ or $p(x_{n-i}|Z_n)$ is obtained, estimates for $\hat{x}_k$ or $\hat{x}_{n-i}$ could be readily determined similar to that discussed in the filtering problem.

Special Case of the Wiener-Kalman Smoothing Problem: In what follows, we shall deal with the problem specification exactly like that of the Wiener-Kalman filter discussed previously, only now, we want the smoothing solution instead. Consider now the following relationships:

$$\left.\begin{aligned} x_{k+1} &= \Phi x_k + w_k \\ z_k &= Hx_k + v_k \end{aligned}\right\} \tag{3.94}$$

where Φ, H are known matrices. Here w_k and v_k are white Gaussian random sequences with zero mean and covariance matrix Q and R, respectively. Using the basic properties of being Gaussian and linear systems, we can obtain the density functions $p(x_{n-i}|Z_n)$ by using Equations 3.93 and 3.94. We proceed by letting i = 1. From Equation 3.93, we have

$$p(x_{n-1}|Z_n) = \frac{p(z_n|x_{n-1}, Z_{n-1})}{p(z_n|Z_{n-1})} p(x_{n-1}|Z_{n-1}) \tag{3.95}$$

The component density functions are

$$\begin{cases} E(z_n|Z_{n-1}) = H\Phi\hat{x}_{n-1|n-1} \\ \operatorname{cov}(z_n|Z_{n-1}) = HP_{n|n-1}H' + R \end{cases}$$

$$P_{n|n-1} \triangleq \Phi P_{n-1|n-1}\Phi' + Q$$

$$\begin{cases} E(z_n|x_{n-1}, Z_{n-1}) = H\Phi x_{n-1} \\ \operatorname{cov}(z_n|x_{n-1}, Z_{n-1}) = HQH' + R \end{cases}$$

$$\begin{cases} E(x_{n-1}|Z_{n-1}) = \hat{x}_{n-1|n-1} \\ \operatorname{cov}(x_{n-1}|Z_{n-1}) = P_{n-1|n-1} \end{cases}$$

Substituting into Equation 3.95 and collecting terms of $||x_{n-1}||^2$ in $p(x_{n-1}|Z_n)$, we obtain

$$P_{n-1|n} = P_{n-1|n-1} + \Phi'H'[HQH' + R]^{-1}H\Phi \tag{3.96}$$

Using the matrix inversion lemma, we have

$$P_{n-1|n} = P_{n-1|n-1} - [P_{n-1|n-1}\Phi' H'(H\Phi P_{n-1|n-1}\Phi' H' + HQH' + R)^{-1} \times H\Phi P_{n-1|n-1}]$$

$$= P_{n-1|n-1} - P_{n-1|n-1}\Phi' H'(HP_{n|n-1}H' + R)^{-1} H\Phi P_{n-1|n-1}$$

$$= P_{n-1|n-1} - P_{n-1|n-1}\Phi' P_{n|n-1}^{-1} P_{n|n-1} H'(HP_{n|n-1}H' + R)^{-1} \times HP_{n|n-1}P_{n|n-1}^{-1}\Phi P_{n-1|n-1}$$

$$= P_{n-1|n-1} + P_{n-1|n-1}\Phi' P_{n|n-1}^{-1}[P_{n|n} - P_{n|n-1}]P_{n|n-1}^{-1}\Phi P_{n-1|n-1}$$

$$= P_{n-1|n-1} + c_{n-1}[P_{n|n} - P_{n|n-1}]c_{n-1}' \tag{3.97}$$

where

$$c_{n-1} \triangleq P_{n-1|n-1}\Phi' P_{n|n-1}^{-1}$$

Taking the cross-product term, we have

$$P_{n-1|n}^{-1}\hat{x}_{n-1|n} = P_{n-1|n-1}^{-1}\hat{x}_{n-1|n-1} + \Phi' H'(HQH' + R)^{-1} z_n$$

Therefore,

$$\hat{x}_{n-1|n} = P_{n-1|n}[P_{n-1|n-1}^{-1}\hat{x}_{n-1|n-1} + \Phi' H'(HQH' + R)^{-1} z_n]$$

$$= \hat{x}_{n-1|n-1} + P_{n-1|n}\Phi' H'(HQH' + R)^{-1}[z_n - H\Phi\hat{x}_{n-1|n-1}] \times [z_n - H\Phi\hat{x}_{n-1|n-1}]$$

$$= \hat{x}_{n-1|n-1} + P_{n-1|n-1}\Phi' H'(H\Phi P_{n-1|n-1}\Phi' H' + HQH' + R)^{-1}$$

$$= \hat{x}_{n-1|n-1} + P_{n-1|n-1}\Phi' P_{n|n-1}^{-1} P_{n|n-1} H'(HP_{n|n-1}H' + R)^{-1} \times [z_n - H\Phi\hat{x}_{n-1|n-1}]$$

$$= \hat{x}_{n-1|n-1} + c_{n-1}[\hat{x}_{n|n} - \Phi\hat{x}_{n-1|n-1}] \tag{3.98}$$

Continuing in this manner inductively, for $i = 2, 3, \cdots$, we obtain the following expression, letting $k \triangleq n - i$,

$$\hat{x}_{k|n} = \hat{x}_{k|k} + P_{k|k}\Phi' P_{k+1|k}[\hat{x}_{k+1|n} - \Phi\hat{x}_{k|k}] \tag{3.99}$$

where

$$P_{k|k} = \Phi^{-1}[P_{k+1|k} - Q]\Phi^{-1'}$$

$$P_{k|k-1}^{-1} = P_{k|k}^{-1} - H'R^{-1}H$$

$$\hat{x}_{k|k} = \Phi^{-1}\hat{x}_{k+1|k+1} - \Phi^{-1}P_{k+1|k}H'R^{-1}[z_{k+1} - H\hat{x}_{k+1|k+1}]$$

3.7 A Simple Nonlinear Non-Gaussian Estimation Problem

The discussions in the previous sections have been carried out in terms of continuous density functions. However, it is obvious that the same process can be applied to problems involving discrete density function and discontinuous functional relationships. It is worthwhile, at this point, to carry out one such solution for a simple, contrived example which nevertheless illustrates some points.

The problem we shall consider can be visualized as an abstraction of the following physical estimation problem: An infrared detector followed by a threshold device is used in a satellite to detect hot targets on the ground. However, extraneous signals, particularly reflection from clouds, obscure the measurements. The problem is to design a multistage estimation process to estimate the presence of hot targets on the ground through measurement of the output of the threshold detector.

Let s_k (target) be a scalar independent Bernoulli process with

$$p(s_k) = (1 - q)\delta(s_k) + q\delta(1 - s_k)\dagger \tag{3.100}$$

Further let n_k (cloud noise) be a scalar Markov process with

$$p(n_1) = (1 - a)\delta(n_1) + a\delta(1 - n_1) \tag{3.101}$$

$$p(n_{k+1}|n_k) = \left(1 - a - \frac{n_k}{2}\right)\delta(n_{k+1}) + \left(a + \frac{n_k}{2}\right)\delta(1 - n_{k+1}) \tag{3.102}$$

and the scalar measurement,

---

†For simplicity, we use the notation that

$$\delta(x) = \begin{cases} 1 & x = 0 \\ 0 & x \neq 0 \end{cases}$$

and p(x) is to be interpreted as mass functions.

$$z_k = s_k \oplus n_k \tag{3.103}$$

where $\oplus$ indicates the logical "or" operation.

Essentially, Equations 3.100 to 3.102 indicate that as the detector sweeps across the field of view, cloud reflection tends to appear in groups while targets appear in isolated dots. See Table 3.1.

Table 3.1. Probability Table

n_1	0	0	1	1
s_1	0	1	0	1
z_1	0	1	1	1
$p(z_1)$	$(1 - a)(1 - q)$	$q(1 - a)$	$a(1 - q)$	aq

Therefore,

$$p(z_1) = (1 - a)(1 - q)\delta(z_1) + (a + q - aq)\delta(z_1 - 1) \tag{3.104}$$

Also,

$$p(z_1|n_1) = \delta(z_1 - 1)n_1 + [(1 - q)\delta(z_1) + q\delta(z_1 - 1)](1 - n_1) \tag{3.105}$$

Then by direct calculation,

$$p(n_1|z_1) = \frac{p(z_1|n_1)p(n_1)}{p(z_1)}$$

$$= [1 - a^1(z_1)]\,\delta(n_1) + a^1(z_1)\delta(n_1 - 1) \tag{3.106}$$

where

$$a^1(z_1) \triangleq \frac{a\delta(z_1 - 1)}{(1 - a)(1 - q)\delta(z_1) + (a + q - aq)\delta(z_1 - 1)} \tag{3.107}$$

Similarly,

$$p(z_1|s_1) = \delta(z_1 - 1)s_1 + [(1 - a)\delta(z_1) + a\delta(z_1 - 1)](1 - s_1) \tag{3.108}$$

and

$$p(s_1|z_1) = \frac{p(z_1|s_1)p(s_1)}{p(z_1)}$$

$$= [1 - q^1(z_1)]\,\delta(s_1) + q^1(z_1)\delta(s_1 - 1) \tag{3.109}$$

where

$$q^1(z_1) = \frac{q\delta(z_1 - 1)}{(1 - a)(1 - q)\delta(z_1) + (a + q - aq)\delta(z_1 - 1)} \tag{3.110}$$

and a reasonable estimate is

$$\hat{s}_1 = \left\{ \begin{array}{ll} 1 & \text{if} \quad q^1(z_1) > \epsilon \\ 0 & \text{if} \quad q^1(z_1) < \epsilon \end{array} \right\} \tag{3.111}$$

where ϵ is a given constant.

Now consider that a second measurement z_2 has been made. We have

$$p(n_2|z_1) = \int_{-\infty}^{\infty} p(n_2|n_1)p(n_1|z_1)\, dn_1$$

which after straightforward, but somewhat laborious, manipulations becomes

$$p(n_2|z_1) = \left(1 - a - \frac{a^1(z_1)}{2}\right)\delta(n_2) + \left(\frac{a^1(z_1)}{2} + a\right)\delta(n_2 - 1)$$

$$\triangleq [1 - a(z_1)]\,\delta(n_2) + a(z_1)\delta(n_2 - 1) \tag{3.112}$$

Furthermore,

$$p(s_2|z_1) \triangleq p(s_2) = (1 - q)\delta(s_2) + q\delta(s_2 - 1) \tag{3.113}$$

Equations 3.112 and 3.113 now take the place of Equations 3.100 and 3.101, and by the same process we can get, in general,

$$p(n_k|Z_k) \triangleq p(n_k|z_k, z_{n-1}, \cdots)$$

$$= [1 - a^1(z_k)]\delta(n_k) + a^1(z_k)\delta(n_k - 1) \tag{3.114}$$

where

$$a^1(z_k) \triangleq a^1(z_k, z_{k-1}, \cdots)$$

$$= \frac{a(z_{k-1})\delta(z_k - 1)}{[1 - a(z_{k-1})](1 - q)\delta(z_k) + [a(z_{k-1}) + q - a(z_{k-1})q]\,\delta(z_k - 1)} \tag{3.115}$$

$$a(z_{k-1}) \triangleq a(z_{k-1}, z_{k-2}, \cdots)$$

$$= a + \frac{a^1(z_{k-1})}{2} \tag{3.116}$$

$$p(s_k|Z_k) \triangleq p(s_k|z_k, z_{k-1}, \cdots)$$

$$= [1 - q^1(z_k)]\,\delta(s_k) + q^1(z_k)\,\delta(s_k - 1) \tag{3.117}$$

$$q^1(z_k) \triangleq q^1(z_k, z_{k-1}, \cdots)$$

$$= \frac{q\delta(z_k - 1)}{[1 - a(z_{k-1})](1 - q)\delta(z_k) + [a(z_{k-1}) + q - a(z_{k-1})q]\delta(z_k - 1)} \tag{3.118}$$

$$p(n_{k+1}|n_k) = [1 - a(z_k)]\delta(n_{k+1}) + a(z_k)\delta(n_{k+1} - 1) \tag{3.119}$$

$$p(s_{k+1}|Z_k) = p(s_{k+1}) \tag{3.120}$$

Equations 3.115 to 3.120 now represent the general solution for the multistage estimation process.

As a check, we consider two possible observed sequences for z, namely (0, 1) and (1, 1). With $a = 1/4$ and $q = 1/4$, we found that $p(s_2|z_2, z_1) = 0.571$ and 0.383, respectively. This agrees with intuition since the sequence (1, 1) has a higher probability of being cloud reflections. On the other hand, the numbers also showed that, under the circumstances, it is very difficult to detect targets with accuracy using the system contrived here. Often, we are actually interested in $p(s_k|z_{k+t})$ with $t > 0$ in order to obtain the so called "smoothed" estimate for s_k. The desired density function can be computed from $p(s_k|z_k)$ by further manipulations. However, the calculation becomes involved and will not be done here.

3.8 Summary

In this chapter, various optimal estimation techniques were introduced. The Wiener filter was first discussed. It was shown that in the case of the Wiener filter, we used the minimum mean-square error as the optimization criterion, and the resultant necessary condition for optimality is given by the famous Wiener-Hopf integral equation. In Section 3.2, we discussed the Wiener-Kalman filter. Kalman, using the concepts of state, reformulated the Wiener filter in a slightly different light and showed that the unbiased, minimum variance estimator must satisfy a set of ordinary differential equations. Notice that Kalman's results were not restricted to stationary cases; however, the restriction of the rational spectrum still must be enforced since this is equivalent to the Markov assumption necessary in the "state" viewpoint. In Section 3.3, the discrete case of the Wiener-Kalman filter was derived using the ordinary calculus. Furthermore, the results obtained could be extended to obtain the optimal smoothing solution which agrees with that of Rauch, Tung, and Striebel[50] obtained by the method of maximum likelihood.† All the results obtained in Section 3.3 are presented as recursive relations for efficient computation. In Section 3.4 the general method of least squares was introduced. It was shown that using the matrix inversion lemma, the successive least-squares fit solutions could be written in a recursive form which is quite efficient for real time computation. Given a dynamic interpretation to the ordinary least-squares fit problem, Bryson and Ho[9, 20] show that the Wiener-Kalman filter can again be derived.

In Section 3.1 through 3.4, it was shown that most of the basic optimization techniques presented in Chapter 2 could be employed for optimal estimation. In Section 3.5, the classical method of maximum likelihood estimation (MLE) was discussed. It was shown that in the case of linear system with Gaussian noise, the MLE is the same as that obtained in the least-squares fit problem discussed in Section 3.4. In Section 3.6, the stochastic estimation problem is approached from a slightly different view point, namely the Bayesian approach.[23] It is an attempt to develop a unified methodology for the general estimation problem. The basic idea of the Bayesian approach is that for all estimation problems the key to the solution is the <u>a posteriori</u> conditional density function $p(x|z)$. Once $p(x|z)$ is obtained, various optimal estimates (that is, most probable, minimax, and so forth) could be readily derived. Section 3.6 shows how the <u>a posteriori</u> conditional density function $p(x|z)$ could be obtained either analytically, or experimentally using the Bayes theorem. It was shown that the Wiener-Kalman filtering and smoothing solution could be readily derived. In Section 3.7 a simple nonlinear, non-Gaussian example was also presented to demonstrate that this concept could be extended to nonlinear cases. It is interesting to note that the most probable estimate (MPE) in the Bayesian approach is, in general, different from that obtained via the classical maximum likelihood, since the latter maximizes the likelihood function $L(x, z)$ with res-

---

†Rauch, Tung, and Striebel did not use the classical MLE, but rather the MLE in the Bayesian sense.

pect to x, whereas the Bayesian approach (MPE) maximizes the product of L(x, z) and p(x) which is the a priori density function of x. If there exists no a priori information, then we assume that all x are equally likely, (that is, zero mean, infinite variance in the Gaussian case), then the two estimates are identical. If a priori information exists, then the estimate obtained via the Bayesian approach will be biased by this information, as it should be. Although, conceptually, the Bayesian approach can be applied to general estimation problems, it does not alleviate all the computation problems. The difficulties associated with the solution of the general problem now appear more specifically as difficulties in steps leading to the computation of $p(x|z)$. These difficulties are

1. Computation of $p(z|x)$. In both the single-stage or multistage case, this problem is complicated by the nonlinear functional relationships between z and x. Except in the case when z and x are linearly related or when z and x are scalars, very little can be done in general, analytically or experimentally. This problem becomes even more difficult if the noise is not additive.
2. Requirement that $p(x|z)$ be in analytical form. This is an obvious requirement if we intend to use the solution in real-time applications. It will not be feasible to compute $p(x|z)$ after z has occurred.
3. For efficient, (recursive) real-time computations, we further require that $p(x)$, $p(x|z)$ be conjugate distributions.† This is simply the requirement that $p(x)$ and $p(x|z)$ be density functions from the same family. Note that all the examples discussed in this chapter possess this desirable property. This is precisely the reason that multistage computation can be done efficiently. In our problem, this imposed a further restriction on the functions g, f, and h.

The difficulties 1 to 3 listed here are formidable ones. It is not likely that we can easily circumvent them except for special class of problems such as those discussed.

It is believed that the unified methodology of the Bayesian approach helps pinpoint these difficulties so that researches toward their solution can then be effectively initiated. Finally, it is felt that the Bayesian approach offers a unified and intuitive viewpoint particularly adaptable to handle modern-day control problems, where the state and the Markov assumptions play a fundamental role.

---

†See Reference 49, Chapter 3.

Chapter 4

IDENTIFICATION

In order to design a satisfactory control system capable of handling a variable dynamic process throughout its operating range, we must either directly or indirectly identify the process dynamics. Numerous schemes and techniques have been developed in recent years that automatically identify the process dynamics and derive a suitable control system. These systems are often referred to as "adaptive control systems" and have found some interesting applications especially in aerospace technology. For example the system developed by Honeywell Inc. that uses the high-grain principle[36, 37, 42] has found practical applications in the X-15, DynaSoar, and some experimental missile systems. Others such as the model reference system developed by the M.I.T. Instrumentation Laboratory[41, 45] and the impluse response identification techniques developed by Aeroneutronics Inc.[56] have also gone through extensive flight-test evaluations. In this chapter, we confine ourselves to the problem of direct identification of system dynamic parameters in a stochastic environment, such as, an aircraft flying through extreme random turbulences, and so forth. By using this method, we imply that the identification process is separated from the derivation of the control law. In other words, we identify first and then use the information obtained to derive the appropriate control law. In general, this type of approach is justifiably open to question; however, we shall develop the techniques first and then evaluate its relative merits later.

The techniques for identifying linear-system parameters are numerous in the literature. Some of the more recent contributions are those of Kalman[29] and Kopp and Orford[34] that enlarge the state space to include the structural parameters and then use perturbation theory and the Kalman filter for state estimation. Kopp and Orford[34] have applied this basic concept to the design of a simple second-order system and have obtained excellent simulation results. Many authors[1, 27, 40, 43, 54] have investigated the identification techniques using cross correlation with varying degrees of success. Numerous other techniques were also developed. Many are summarized and discussed in References 15 and 43. In this work, the basic concept employed is the familiar "least-squares fit" over finite data. The emphasis is on the simplicity of computation. The basic theory is first developed under various conditions. It is shown that the resultant scheme is deterministic and is optimal in the least-squares sense. When given a stochastic interpretation, it is shown that the estimation scheme is statistically consistent. The computational schemes developed are employed in the identification of second- and fourth-order system parameters with excellent results.

4.1 General Mathematical Preliminaries

4.1.1 Basic Mathematical Models. Consider a dynamic system whose behavior can be described by a set of linear differential equations,

$$\mathring{x} = F(t)x + G(t)u \qquad x_0 \text{ given} \tag{4.1}$$

where x is the state vector and u the control vector; $F(t)$, $G(t)$ may be time varying. Then according to the theory of linear differential equations, all solutions to these equations are expressible in terms of the so-called fundamental matrix solutions $\Phi(t, t_0)$ (transition matrix). Then $\Phi(t, t_0)$ satisfies the equation

$$\frac{d}{dt}\Phi(t, t_0) = F(t)\,\Phi(t, t_0) \qquad \Phi(t_0, t_0) = I \tag{4.2}$$

and the solution to Equation 4.1 is

$$x(t) = \Phi(t, t_0)x_0 + \int_{t_0}^{t} \Phi(t, \tau)G(\tau)u(\tau)\,d\tau \tag{4.3}$$

To compute $\Phi(t, \tau)$ for variable τ, we employ the adjoint equation

$$\frac{d}{d\tau}\Phi'(t, \tau) = -F'(\tau)\,\Phi'(t, \tau) \qquad \Phi'(\tau, \tau) = I$$

where t is fixed.

In the following, all computational schemes are developed for digital computation. We shall convert the earlier relationships to their discrete equivalent. Once the sampled period T is fixed and assuming that the control is piecewise constant, $u(t) = u(i)$ for $iT \le t \le (i + 1)T$, we have

$$x(i + 1) = \Phi(i + 1, i)\,x(i) + D(i)u(i)$$

where

$$\Phi(i + 1, i) \triangleq \Phi[(i + 1)T, iT]$$

$$D(i) \triangleq \int_{iT}^{(i+1)T} \Phi[(i+1)T, t]\, G(t)\, dt$$

For the case of stationary, constant coefficient, systems, we have simply

$$x(i+1) = \Phi x(i) + Du(i)$$

In general, the matrix block diagram of the system is represented in Figure 4.1. In practice, not all the state variables can be

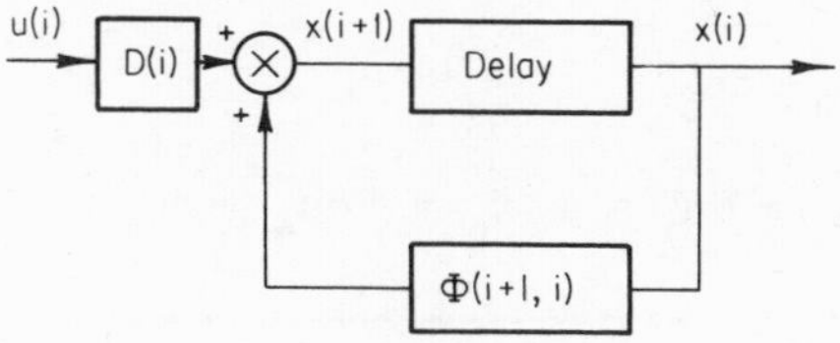

Figure 4.1. Matrix block diagram.

measured directly; hence, we have an additional equation

$$z(i) = H(i)x(i) + v(i)$$

where z is the measurement vector $(m \times 1)$, H is an $m \times n$ matrix, and v is a measurement noise vector $(m \times 1)$. Hence the block diagram, Figure 4.1, becomes Figure 4.2.

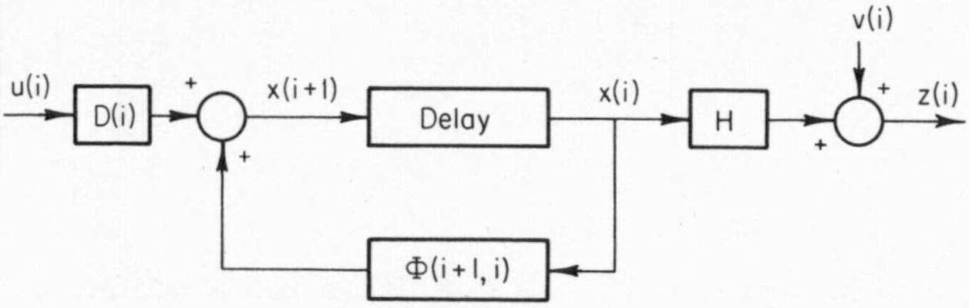

Figure 4.2. Matrix block diagram.

4.1.2 Controllability, Observability, and Identifiability of Stationary Linear Systems. The concepts of controllability, observability, and identifiability define some fundamental characteristics of linear systems. If these conditions are not met, optimal control, estimation, and identification cannot be obtained. These concepts were first introduced by Kalman and others for continuous systems. In the following, we will present a discrete equivalent of these conditions.

Controllability Condition:

Given:

$$x_{k+1} = \Phi x_k + du_k \qquad \text{u is a scalar, x is a n-vector}$$

$$x_i \triangleq x(i) \qquad x_0 \text{ given}$$

Question: Under what condition can we determine the control necessary to drive the system to x_n, where x_n is arbitrary in the state space?

Solution:

$$x_1 = \Phi x_0 + du_0$$

$$x_2 = \Phi x_1 + du_1 = \Phi^2 x_0 + \Phi du_0 + du_1$$

$$\vdots$$

$$x_n = \Phi^n x_0 + \Phi^{n-1} du_0 + \Phi^{n-2} du_1 + \cdots + du_{n-1}$$

Therefore,

$$x_n - \Phi^n x_0 = \Phi^{n-1} du_0 + \Phi^{n-2} du_1 + \cdots + du_{n-1}$$

$$= \left[d \;\vdots\; \Phi d \;\vdots\; \cdots \;\vdots\; \Phi^{n-1} d \right] \begin{bmatrix} u_{n-1} \\ u_{n-2} \\ \vdots \\ u_1 \\ u_0 \end{bmatrix}$$

Since x_n and x_0 are given, the condition for a unique solution to exist is

$$\left[d \;\vdots\; \Phi d \;\vdots\; \cdots \;\vdots\; \Phi^{n-1} d \right] \quad \text{has rank n}$$

If this condition is satisfied, then Φ, d is called a controllable pair. For the case where u is a vector, the extension is straight-forward.

Observability Condition:

Given:

$$x_{k+1} = \Phi x_k \qquad x_0 \text{ given}$$

$$z_k = h' x_k \qquad \text{z scalar}$$

Question: Under what condition can we determine the x's by observing the z's?

Solution:

$$z_0 = h'x_0$$

$$z_1 = h'\Phi x_0$$

$$\vdots$$

$$z_{n-1} = h'\Phi^{n-1}x_0$$

Therefore,

$$\begin{bmatrix} z_0 \\ z_1 \\ \vdots \\ z_n \end{bmatrix} = \begin{bmatrix} h' \\ h'\Phi \\ \vdots \\ h'\Phi^{n-1} \end{bmatrix} x_0 \equiv Ax_0$$

If x_0 is to be determined uniquely, A must be nonsingular. The observability condition is the matrix

$$\begin{bmatrix} h' \\ h'\Phi \\ \vdots \\ h'\Phi^{n-1} \end{bmatrix} \quad \text{has rank n (nonsingular)}$$

If this condition is satisfied, then (Φ, h) is called an observable pair. Using the same argument, it follows that if A is nonsingular, we can determine all the states $x_0, x_1, \cdots, x_i$ by taking appropriate measurement, z's. The extension to the case where z is a vector follows in a straightforward manner.

n-Identifiability Condition:
Given: a free dynamic system,

$$x_{k+1} = \Phi x_k \qquad x_0 \text{ given}$$

Question: If all the states can be observed, under what conditions can Φ be identified (determined)?

Solution: Let

$$x_1 = \Phi x_0$$

$$x_2 = \Phi x_1 = \Phi^2 x_0$$

$$\vdots$$

$$x_n = \Phi x_{n-1} = \Phi^{n-1} x_0$$

Since all the state variables can be observed, we can set up a matrix after n measurements:

$$\left[x_1 \,\vdots\, x_2 \,\vdots\, x_3 \,\vdots\, \cdots \,\vdots\, x_n \right] = \left[\Phi x_0 \,\vdots\, \Phi x_1 \,\vdots\, \cdots \,\vdots\, \Phi x_{n-1} \right]$$

$$= \Phi \left[x_0 \,\vdots\, x_1 \,\vdots\, \cdots \,\vdots\, x_{n-1} \right]$$

If Φ is to be determined uniquely, the matrix

$$\left[x_0 \,\vdots\, x_1 \,\vdots\, \cdots \,\vdots\, x_{n-1} \right]$$

must be nonsingular. Consequently, we can define the n-identifiability matrix as

$$B \triangleq \left[x_0 \,\vdots\, x_1 \,\vdots\, x_2 \,\vdots\, \cdots \,\vdots\, x_{n-1} \right] \equiv \left[x_0 \,\vdots\, \Phi x_0 \,\vdots\, \cdots \,\vdots\, \Phi^{n-1} x_0 \right]$$

and the system is said to be n-identifiable if the matrix B is nonsingular. Physically, this condition implies that x_0 must excite all modes of the system.

Physical Interpretation: We can give a definite physical interpretation of the controllability, observability, identifiability condition by proceeding via the following approach. Consider first the controllability condition for the system

$$x_{k+1} = \Phi x_k + d u_k$$

Performing a similarity transformation, we have†

$$y_{k+1} = A^{-1} x_{k+1}$$

Therefore,

†For simplicity, Φ is assumed to have real and distinct eigenvalues.

$$y_{k+1} = A^{-1}\Phi A y_k + A^{-1} d u_k$$

$$= \begin{bmatrix} \lambda_1 & & & \\ & \lambda_2 & & \\ & & \ddots & \\ & & & \lambda_n \end{bmatrix} y_k + d_1 u_k$$

Now, we have n uncoupled equations representing the n basic modes of the system. If u is to excite all modes of the system, the vector d_1 must not have any zero components. From elementary matrix theory, we have

$$A^{-1} \equiv \begin{bmatrix} e_1{*'} \\ e_2{*'} \\ \vdots \\ e_n{*'} \end{bmatrix}$$

where $e*'$ s are conjugate eigenvectors. Hence if d_1 is to have nontrivial components, the vector d must be made up of nontrivial linear combinations of all the eigenvectors of Φ. In other words, the vector d must have nontrivial projections to all eigenvectors such that it is capable of exciting all modes of the system. Consequently, an alternate definition of controllability is that the vector d must be expressible in terms of nontrivial linear combinations of the eigenvectors of Φ. The derivation for observability and identifiability follows in analogous manner. Physically, this implies that if the system is observable, we must be able to see all modes of the system. If the system is identifiable, then the initial condition must have nontrivial projections on to all the eigenvectors of Φ so as to excite all modes of the system.

4.1.3 Standard Transformations. Before we can proceed to discuss the identification problem, the following standard transformations are necessary: The first transforms any Φ, h pair into its canonical equivalent pair Φ^*, h^*. The second transforms a difference equation into the canonical form Φ^*, h^* and vice versa.

Standard canonical transformation 1. Given a dynamic system

$$\left.\begin{aligned} x_{k+1} &= \Phi x_k + \Gamma w_k \qquad x_0 \text{ given} \\ z_k &= h' x_k \end{aligned}\right\} \tag{4.3}$$

Proposition 4.1: Given any observable pair Φ, h, they can be transformed to the canonical form Φ^*, h^* by using the observability matrix A, where A, Φ^*, h^* are defined,

$$\Phi^* \triangleq \left[\begin{array}{c|c} 0 & \\ 0 & \\ \vdots & I \\ 0 & \\ \hline \multicolumn{2}{c}{\phi'} \end{array}\right]$$

$$h^* \triangleq \begin{bmatrix} 1 \\ 0 \\ \vdots \\ 0 \end{bmatrix}$$

$$A = \begin{bmatrix} h' \\ h'\Phi \\ \vdots \\ h'\Phi^{n-1} \end{bmatrix}$$

where ϕ is a vector whose components are to be determined.

Transformation: Let

$$y_k = Ax_k$$

Therefore,

$$x_k = A^{-1} y_k \tag{4.4}$$

Substituting Equation 4.4 into 4.3, we have

$$y_{k+1} = A\Phi A^{-1} y_k + A\Gamma w_k$$

$$\triangleq \Phi^* y_k + \Gamma_1 w_k$$

$$z_k = h' A^{-1} y_k$$

$$\triangleq h^{*'} y_k \tag{4.5}$$

<u>Proof</u>:

$$A\Phi A^{-1} = \begin{bmatrix} h' \\ \hdashline h'\Phi \\ \vdots \\ h'\Phi^{n-1} \end{bmatrix} \Phi \begin{bmatrix} h' \\ \hdashline h'\Phi \\ \vdots \\ h'\Phi^{n-1} \end{bmatrix}^{-1}$$

$$= \begin{bmatrix} h' \\ h'\Phi \\ \vdots \\ h'\Phi^{n-2} \\ \hdashline h'\Phi^{n-1} \end{bmatrix} I \begin{bmatrix} h'\Phi^{-1} \\ \hdashline h' \\ \vdots \\ h'\Phi^{n-2} \end{bmatrix}^{-1}$$

$$\triangleq \begin{bmatrix} D \\ \hdashline d' \end{bmatrix} \begin{bmatrix} e' \\ \hdashline D \end{bmatrix}^{-1}$$

$$= \begin{bmatrix} D \\ \hdashline d' \end{bmatrix} \begin{bmatrix} e_{-1} & \vdots & D_{-1} \end{bmatrix}$$

$$= \begin{bmatrix} 0 & \vdots & \\ 0 & \vdots & \\ \vdots & \vdots & I \\ 0 & \vdots & \\ \hdashline d'e_{-1} & \vdots & d'D_{-1} \end{bmatrix} \equiv \Phi^*$$

where we have defined

$$\begin{bmatrix} e' \\ \hdashline D \end{bmatrix}^{-1} \triangleq \left[e_{-1} \;\middle|\; D_{-1} \right]$$

Therefore,

$$e'e_{-1} = 1 \qquad e'D_{-1} = [0\ 0 \cdots 0]$$

$$De_{-1} = \begin{bmatrix} 0 \\ 0 \\ \vdots \\ 0 \end{bmatrix} \qquad DD_{-1} = [I]$$

Similarly,

$$h'A^{-1} = h' \begin{bmatrix} h' \\ h'\Phi \\ \vdots \\ h'\Phi^{n-1} \end{bmatrix}^{-1}$$

$$= [h'\Phi^{-1}] \begin{bmatrix} h'\Phi^{-1} \\ h' \\ \vdots \\ h'\Phi^{n-2} \end{bmatrix}^{-1}$$

$$= [h'\Phi^{-1}] \begin{bmatrix} e' \\ \hdashline D \end{bmatrix}^{-1}$$

$$= [e'] \left[e_{-1} \;\middle|\; D_{-1} \right]$$

$$= \left[e'e_{-1} \;\middle|\; e'D_{-1} \right]$$

$$= \left[1, 0, 0, 0, 0, 0 \right]$$

$$= h^{*'}$$

QED

This transformation implies that as far as the input w_k and output z_k are concerned, the two systems in Figure 4.3 are completely equivalent,

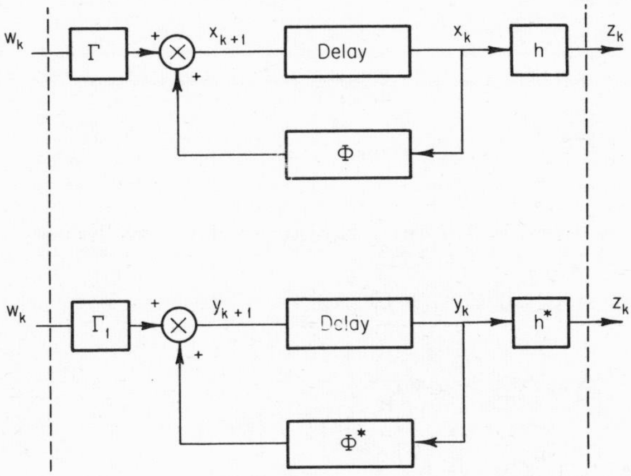

Figure 4.3. Equivalent linear systems.

where

$$y_0 = Ax_0$$

$$\Phi^* = A\Phi A^{-1} = \left[\begin{array}{c|c} 0 & \\ 0 & I \\ 0 & \\ \hline \multicolumn{2}{c}{\Phi'} \end{array}\right]$$

$$h^{*\prime} = h' A^{-1} = [1, 0, 0, 0, 0]$$

$$\Gamma_1 = A\Gamma$$

Proposition 4.2: Given any controllable pair Φ, d, they can be transformed to the modified canonical form Φ^{**} and d^* by using the controllability matrix C. Then Φ^{**}, d^*, C are defined,

$$C = \left[d \mid \Phi d \mid \cdots \mid \Phi^{n-1} d \right] \qquad \text{an } n \times n \text{ matrix}$$

$$\Phi^{**} = \left[\begin{array}{ccccc|c} 0 & 0 & 0 & 0 & 0 & \\ \hline & & I & & & \phi \\ & & & & & \end{array}\right] \qquad d^* = \begin{bmatrix} 1 \\ 0 \\ \vdots \\ 0 \end{bmatrix}$$

Transformation:

Let

$$y_k = C^{-1} x_k \tag{4.6}$$

Therefore,

$$x_k = C y_k \tag{4.7}$$

Substituting Equation 4.7 into Equation 4.6, we have

$$y_{k+1} = C^{-1} \Phi C y_k + C^{-1} d u_k$$

$$\triangleq \Phi^{**} y_k + d^* u_k$$

$$z_k = h' C y_k \triangleq h_1' y_k$$

where

$$\Phi^{**} = C^{-1} \Phi C \qquad d^* = C^{-1} d$$

Proof: The proof is entirely analogous to that of Proposition 4.1.

Standard transformation 2. Given a difference equation

$$z_k + a_1 z_{k-1} + a_2 z_{k-2} + \cdots + a_n z_{k-n} = b_1 u_{k-1} + b_2 u_{k-2} + \cdots + b_n u_{k-n}$$

It can be reduced to the standard canonical form Φ^*, h^* given

$$x(k) = \Phi^* x(k - 1) + d u(k - 1)$$

$$z_k = h^{*\prime} x(k)$$

where

$$\Phi^* = \left[\begin{array}{c|c} 0 & \\ 0 & \\ \vdots & I \\ 0 & \\ \hline \multicolumn{2}{c}{-a_n, -a_{n-1}, \cdots, -a_1} \end{array}\right]$$

$$d = \begin{bmatrix} 1 & & & & 0 \\ a_1 & 1 & & & \\ a_2 & a_1 & 1 & & \\ \vdots & \vdots & \vdots & \ddots & \\ a_{n-1} & a_{n-2} & \cdots & & 1 \end{bmatrix}^{-1} \begin{bmatrix} b_1 \\ b_2 \\ \vdots \\ b_n \end{bmatrix}$$

$$h^* = \begin{bmatrix} 1 \\ 0 \\ 0 \\ \vdots \\ 0 \end{bmatrix}$$

where the x's and z's are related as follows:

$$x_1(k) = z_k$$

$$x_2(k) = z_{k+1} - d_1 u(k)$$

$$x_3(k) = z_{k+2} - d_1 u(k+1) - d_2 u(k)$$

$$\vdots$$

$$x_n(k) = z_{k+n-1} - d_1 u(k+n-2) - d_2 u(k+n-3) - \cdots - d_{n-1} u(k)$$

The detailed derivation is as follows: <u>Given</u> a difference equation,

$$z_k + a_1 z_{k-1} + a_2 z_{k-2} + \cdots + a_n z_{k-n} = b_1 u_{k-1} + b_2 u_{k-2} + \cdots + b_n u_{k-n} \tag{4.8}$$

we wish to reduce this to the standard form

$$\left. \begin{aligned} x(k) &= \Phi^* x(k-1) + du(k-1) \\ z_k &= h^{*\prime} x(k) \end{aligned} \right\} \tag{4.9}$$

<u>Solution</u>: By direct substitution, we have

$$x_1(k) = z_k$$

$$x_1(k) = x_2(k-1) + d_1 u(k-1)$$

$$x_2(k) = x_3(k-1) + d_2 u(k-1)$$

$$\vdots$$

$$x_{n-1}(k) = x_n(k-1) + d_{n-1} u(k-1)$$

$$x_n(k) = -a_n x_1(k-1) - a_{n-1} x_2(k-1) - \cdots - a_1 x_n(k-1) + d_n u(k-1) \tag{4.10}$$

Rearranging Equation 4.10, we have

$$x_2(k-1) = x_1(k) - d_1 u(k-1) = z_k - d_1 u(k-1)$$

$$x_3(k-1) = x_2(k) - d_2 u(k-1) = z_{k+1} - d_1 u(k) - d_2 u(k-1)$$

$$\vdots$$

$$x_n(k-1) = x_{n-1}(k) - d_{n-1} u(k-1) = z_{k+n-2} - d_1 u(k+n-3) - \cdots - d_{n-1} u(k-1) \tag{4.11}$$

Therefore, it follows that

$$x_n(k) = z_{k+n-1} - d_1 u(k+n-2) - \cdots - d_{n-1} u(k)$$

Putting Equation 4.11 equal to the last of Equation 4.10, we have

$$\begin{aligned} z_{k+n-1} &- d_1 u(k+n-2) - d_2 u(k+n-3) - \cdots - d_{n-1} u(k) \\ &= -a_n x_1(k-1) - a_{n-1} x_2(k-1) - \cdots - a_1 x_{n-1}(k-1) + d_n u(k-1) \\ &= -a_n z_{k-1} - a_{n-1}[z_k - d_1 u(k-1)] - a_{n-2}[z_{k+1} - d_1 u(k) - d_2 u(k-1)] \\ &\quad - a_1[z_{k+n-2} - d_1 u(k+n-3) - \cdots - d_{n-1} u(k-1)] \\ &\quad + d_n u(k-1) \end{aligned} \tag{4.12}$$

Rearranging Equation 4.12 and lowering the index by n - 1, we have

$$\begin{aligned} z_k &+ a_1 z_{k-1} + a_2 z_{k-2} + \cdots + a_{n-1} z_{k-n+1} + a_n z_{k-n} \\ &= d_1 u(k-1) + d_2 u(k-2) + \cdots + d_{n-1} u(k-n+1) + d_n u(k-n) \end{aligned}$$

$$+ a_{n-1} d_1 u(k - n) + a_{n-2}[d_1 u(k - n + 1) + d_2 u(k - n)] - \cdots$$

$$+ a_1[d_1 u(k - 2) - d_2 u(k - 3) - \cdots - d_{n-1} u(k - n)]$$

$$= b_1 u_{k-1} + b_2 u_{k-2} + b_3 u_{k-3} + \cdots + b_n u_{k-n} \cdots \tag{4.13}$$

Equating the coefficients in Equation 4.13, we have

$$b_1 = d_1$$

$$b_2 = [d_2 + a_1 d_1]$$

$$b_3 = [d_3 + a_1 d_2 + a_2 d_1]$$

$$\vdots$$

$$b_n = [d_n + a_1 d_{n-1} + a_2 d_{n-2} + \cdots + a_{n-1} d_1]$$

Consequently, we have

$$\begin{bmatrix} d_1 \\ d_2 \\ d_3 \\ \vdots \\ d_n \end{bmatrix} = \begin{bmatrix} 1 & & & & & 0 \\ a_1 & 1 & & & & \\ a_2 & a_1 & 1 & & & \\ a_3 & a_2 & a_1 & 1 & & \\ \vdots & \vdots & \vdots & & \ddots & \\ a_{n-1} & a_{n-2} & a_{n-3} & a_2 & a_1 & 1 \end{bmatrix}^{-1} \begin{bmatrix} b_1 \\ b_2 \\ b_3 \\ \vdots \\ b_n \end{bmatrix} \tag{4.14}$$

and

$$\Phi * = \left[\begin{array}{c|c} 0 & \\ 0 & \\ 0 & I \\ \vdots & \\ 0 & \\ \hline \multicolumn{2}{c}{-a_n, \ -a_{n-1}, \ \cdots, \ -a_2, \ -a_1} \end{array}\right] \tag{4.15}$$

QED

4.2 Process Identification, Linear System, Deterministic Case

Problem: Consider the free dynamic system (see Figure 4.4).

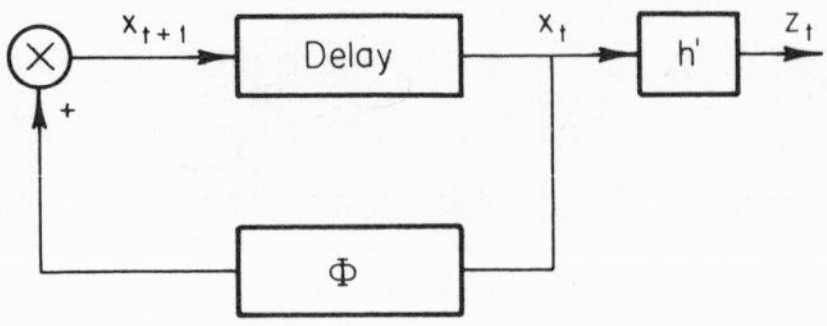

Figure 4.4. Free dynamic system.

$$x_{t+1} = \Phi x_t \tag{4.16}$$

and the scalar measurement

$$z_t = h'x_t \tag{4.17}$$

Under what conditions is it possible to identify the system of Equation 4.16 measurements of z_t alone? We use the word "identification" in the sense meaning that we can determine Φ^*, h^* such that

$$\mathscr{S}_{t+1} = \Phi^* \mathscr{S}_t \tag{4.18}$$

$$z_t = h^{*\prime} \mathscr{S}_t \tag{4.19}$$

where $\mathscr{S}_t$ is some new state vector.

In other words, as far as the output measurable sequence z_t is concerned, there is absolutely no difference between the behavior of the starred and unstarred systems. (This implies that all the eigenvalues or poles of the two systems must be the same.)

4.2.1 Necessary and Sufficient Condition for Identification.

Definition: A system of Equation 4.16 is said to be n-identifiable if it is possible to determine Φ by measurement of all the x variables.

Definition: A system given by Equations 4.16 and 4.17 is said to be 1-identifiable if it is possible to determine Φ^* and h^* such that Equations 4.18 and 4.19 are equivalent to Equations 4.16 and 4.17 in the sense mentioned by measurement of z_t only.

As shown previously, Equation 4.16 is n-identifiable if and only if the matrix

$$\left[x_0 \;\vdots\; \Phi x_0 \;\vdots\; \Phi^2 x_0 \;\vdots\; \cdots \;\vdots\; \Phi^{n-1} x_0 \right]$$

is nonsingular. This means that the initial conditions must excite all modes of the system.

It turns out that the necessary and sufficient condition for the solution of the 1-identification problem is that the system be n-identifiable and that Φ, h be an observable pair. The necessity of this requirement is more or less obvious. If Φ, h is not observable, then we have no hope of ever determining x_t even if Φ is known. Similarly if Φ, x_0 is not an identifiable pair then we cannot determine Φ even if x_t are all measurable. The problem is to show that the combination of these two conditions is sufficient for 1-identifiability. This is done as follows: Let

$$\mathscr{S}_n \triangleq \begin{bmatrix} z_1 \\ z_2 \\ \vdots \\ z_n \end{bmatrix} \tag{4.20}$$

then

$$\mathscr{S}_n = \begin{bmatrix} h'\Phi \\ h'\Phi^2 \\ \vdots \\ h'\Phi^n \end{bmatrix} x_0 \equiv A\Phi x_0 \qquad A \triangleq \begin{bmatrix} h' \\ h'\Phi \\ \vdots \\ h'\Phi^{n-1} \end{bmatrix}$$

Similarly,

$$\mathscr{S}_{n+1} = A\Phi x_1 = A\Phi^2 x_0 \tag{4.21}$$

such that we have

$$S_{2n-1} \triangleq \left[\mathscr{S}_n, \middle| \mathscr{S}_{n+1}, \middle| \cdots, \middle| \mathscr{S}_{2n-1} \right] = \begin{bmatrix} z_1 & z_2 & \cdots & z_n \\ z_2 & z_3 & & z_{n+1} \\ \vdots & \vdots & & \vdots \\ z_n & z_{n+1} & & z_{2n-1} \end{bmatrix}$$

$$= A \left[\Phi x_0 \;\middle|\; \Phi^2 x_0 \;\middle|\; \cdots \;\middle|\; \Phi^n x_0 \right]$$

$$\equiv A\Phi B$$

Therefore,

$$\Phi = A^{-1} S_{2n-1} B^{-1} \tag{4.22}$$

Therefore, the condition for 1-identifiability implies observability and n-identifiability. Since Φ is never singular, (a property of a linear system) observability and identifiability are necessary and sufficient to guarantee the nonsingularity of S_{2n-1}, which also happens to be symmetric.

However, from Equation 4.21, we also have

$$\mathcal{S}_{n+1} = A\Phi^2 x_0 = A\Phi A^{-1}\mathcal{S}_n \triangleq \Phi^*\mathcal{S}_n \tag{4.23}$$

such that Equation 4.23 for different values of the subscripts can be written as

$$S_{2n} = \Phi^* S_{2n-1} \tag{4.24}$$

Thus, because of the nonsingularity of S_{2n-1}, we can write

$$\Phi^* = S_{2n} S^{-1}_{2n-1} \tag{4.25}$$

Now we can directly verify that

$$\mathcal{S}_{t+1} = \Phi^*\mathcal{S}_t \tag{4.26}$$

$$z_t = h^{*\prime}\mathcal{S}_t \tag{4.27}$$

where $h^{*\prime} = (1, 0, \cdots, 0, 0)$ represents the required identification. The state vector x_t is related to the equivalent state vector $\mathcal{S}_t$ by

$$\mathcal{S}_{t+n} = A\Phi x_t \tag{4.28}$$

and

$$\Phi^* = A\Phi A^{-1} \tag{4.29}$$

$$h^* = A^{-1\prime} h \tag{4.30}$$

Note that Φ^* is indeed the canonical form of a single-output discrete system. We let

$$S_{2n} \triangleq \begin{bmatrix} C \\ \hline e' \end{bmatrix} \tag{4.31}$$

Then by definition of the S_i's, we have for S_{2n-1} and S^{-1}_{2n-1}

$$S_{2n-1} \triangleq \begin{bmatrix} d' \\ \hline C \end{bmatrix} \qquad S_{2n-1} = \left[d_{-1} \;\middle|\; C_{-1} \right] \tag{4.32}$$

where

$$\left. \begin{aligned} d'd_{-1} &= 1 \qquad & d'C_{-1} &= 0 \\ CC_{-1} &= I \qquad & Cd_{-1} &= 0 \end{aligned} \right\} \tag{4.33}$$

Consequently, from Equation 4.25,

$$\Phi^* = S_{2n} S^{-1}_{2n-1} = \left[\begin{array}{c|c} 0 & \\ 0 & \\ \vdots & I \\ 0 & \\ \hline e'd_{-1} & e'C^{-1} \end{array} \right] \equiv \left[\begin{array}{c|c} 0 & \\ 0 & \\ \vdots & I \\ 0 & \\ \hline \multicolumn{2}{c}{-a_n, -a_{n-1}, \cdots, -a_1} \end{array} \right] \tag{4.34}$$

Since the elements of e', d_{-1}, C_{-1}, are completely determined by measurement of the z_t's, then Φ^* is always computable. From Equations 4.34 and 4.23, we can see that the output is actually being characterized by a free-difference equation with initial conditions given.

$$z_{n+1} = a_1 z_n + a_2 z_{n-1} + \cdots + a_n z_1 \tag{4.35}$$

In z-transform theory, Equation 4.35 is equivalent to the z-transfer function

$$G(z) = \frac{[\quad]}{1 + a_1 z^{-1} + a_2 z^{-2} + \cdots + a_n z^{-n}} \tag{4.36}$$

Equations 4.29 and 4.30 show the explicit computation of transforming a given Φ, h pair into the canonical pair of Φ^*, h^*.

4.2.2 Identification of Processes When the Order is Unknown. Now, we shall consider the problem where the order of the system is unknown. In other words, we know that the output z_t's at our disposal came from a linear dynamic system but we know neither the parameters nor the order of the system.

Question: Can we determine Φ^*, under such circumstances?

Solution: Although the order of the system is unknown, let us assume that it is less than n, where n is some integer. Analogous to Equation 4.20, form the vectors

$$\mathcal{S}_n = \begin{bmatrix} z_1 \\ z_2 \\ \vdots \\ z_n \end{bmatrix} \qquad \mathcal{S}_{n+1} = \begin{bmatrix} z_2 \\ z_3 \\ \vdots \\ z_{n+1} \end{bmatrix}$$

Now form a $(n \times K)$ matrix,

$$A_k = \left[\mathcal{S}_n \;\vdots\; \mathcal{S}_{n+1} \;\vdots\; \cdots \;\vdots\; \mathcal{S}_{n+k-1} \right] \tag{4.37}$$

and the matrix product $A_k{}' A_k$:

> Proposition 4.3: If the system is of the order m, then the product $A_k{}' A_k$ will be positive definite for $k = 1, 2, \cdots, m$ and will be singular for $k > m$.

Proof: If the system is of order m, then A_n is of rank m† for $n \geq m$ and A_k will be of rank K for all $K \leq m$. Therefore, we can partition A_k as follows:

$$A_k = \begin{bmatrix} B_k \\ \text{-----} \\ C_k \end{bmatrix}$$

where B_k is a nonsingular $K \times K$ matrix. Therefore,

$$A_k{}'A_k = B_k{}'B_k + C_k{}'C_k$$

as long as $K \leq m$. Since B_k is nonsingular, therefore $B_k{}' B_k$ will be positive definite and $C_k{}' C_k$ will be positive semidefinite. Therefore, $A_k{}' A_k$ will be positive definite. (Note: The sum of a positive definite matrix and a positive semidefinite matrix is always positive definite.) Using this technique, we can readily determine the order of the system by starting with $K = 1, 2, \cdots$, until $A_k{}'A_k$ becomes singular. The determinant of Φ^* follows in a straightforward manner.‡

---

†1-identifiability condition.

‡If the system is of order m, it can only span an m-dimensional space. Hence, A_m will be of rank m if the system is 1-identifiable.

4.3 Process Identification, Stochastic Case

4.3.1 Noise Input Only. Consider the following system:

$$\left.\begin{aligned} x_{t+1} &= \Phi x_t + \Gamma w_t \\ z_t &= h' x_t \end{aligned}\right\} \tag{4.38}$$

where w_t is a random noise sequence and cannot be measured.

Problem: Given the measurements $z_1, z_2, \cdots, z_t$, obtain the best estimate of Φ to within a linear transformation.

Solution: We shall begin by assuming that Φ, h is an observable pair (otherwise, identification is meaningless). From Proposition 4.1 of standard transformation 1, then Φ, h, Γ can be transformed into the canonical form of Φ^*, h^*, Γ_1. Using standard transformation 2, then Φ^*, h^*, Γ_1 can in turn be transformed into a difference equation.

$$z_t + a_1 z_{t-1} + a_2 z_{t-2} + \cdots + a_n z_{t-n} = b_1 w_{t-1} + b_2 w_{t-2} + \cdots \tag{4.39}$$

Alternately, we have

$$z_t = \mathscr{S}_{t-1}' \phi + n_{t-1}' b$$

where

$$\phi \triangleq \begin{bmatrix} -a_n \\ -a_{n-1} \\ \vdots \\ -a_2 \\ -a_1 \end{bmatrix} \quad \mathscr{S}_{t-1} \triangleq \begin{bmatrix} z_{t-n} \\ z_{t-n+1} \\ \vdots \\ z_{t-2} \\ z_{t-1} \end{bmatrix} \quad b \triangleq \begin{bmatrix} b_n \\ b_{n-1} \\ \vdots \\ b_2 \\ b_1 \end{bmatrix} \quad n_{t-1} = \begin{bmatrix} w_{t-n} \\ \vdots \\ w_{t-1} \end{bmatrix}$$

At this point, the problem is reduced to identifying n parameters in the vector ϕ which are the coefficients of the difference equation instead of the n^2 parameters necessary to identify the original Φ. As is pointed out in the previous section, these coefficients in ϕ, b are precisely those of the z-transfer function relating the input w_t and the output z_t. To find the solution to this identification problem, let us first consider a special case.

Special case — the vector b has only one nonzero element. Although in most identification problems, we have no information about the character of the vector b, it is assumed that it has only one nonzero element, say b_1 here for the sake of clarity in the derivation. In later sections, the procedure will be extended to handle the cases where b has more nonzero elements. Consider now the following difference equation:

$$z_{t+1} = \mathscr{S}_t' \phi + w_t \tag{4.40}$$

where w_t is a random noise sequence. (For simplicity, b_1 is set equal to 1 with no loss of generality.)

If ϕ is an n vector (n^{th}-order system), then we can readily write down a solution after 2n measurements, assuming z_i are <u>not</u> given for $i \leq 0$, namely,

$$\begin{bmatrix} z_{n+1} \\ z_{n+2} \\ \vdots \\ z_{2n} \end{bmatrix} = \begin{bmatrix} \mathscr{S}_n' \\ \mathscr{S}_{n+1}' \\ \vdots \\ \mathscr{S}_{2n-1}' \end{bmatrix} \phi + \begin{bmatrix} w_n \\ w_{n+1} \\ \vdots \\ w_{2n-1} \end{bmatrix}$$

$$= \begin{bmatrix} z_1 z_2 & \cdots & z_n \\ z_2 z_3 & \cdots & z_{n+1} \\ \vdots & & \vdots \\ z_n z_{n+1} & \cdots & z_{2n-1} \end{bmatrix} \phi + \begin{bmatrix} w_n \\ w_{n+1} \\ \vdots \\ w_{2n-1} \end{bmatrix}$$

Alternately, we have

$$\mathscr{S}_{2n} = \begin{bmatrix} S_{2n-1} \end{bmatrix} \phi + \begin{bmatrix} w_n \\ \vdots \\ w_{2n-1} \end{bmatrix} \tag{4.41}$$

Therefore,

$$\phi = S_{2n-1}^{-1} \mathscr{S}_{2n} + \epsilon \tag{4.42}$$

where the stochastic error vector is

$$\epsilon \triangleq - \begin{bmatrix} \\ S_{2n-1} \\ \\ \end{bmatrix}^{-1} \begin{bmatrix} w_n \\ \vdots \\ w_{2n-1} \end{bmatrix}$$

If the error vector ϵ is zero, Equation 4.42 is a unique solution, if it is not, then $\Phi = [S_{2n-1}]^{-1}\mathcal{S}_{2n}$ is a least-squares solution, since it is the solution that minimizes the norm of the error vector. As we take on more measurements, this can be generalized into the least-squares fit solution (discussed in Section 3.4 of Chapter 3); namely, choose Φ to minimize

$$J = \sum_{n+1}^{t} \| w_{i-1} \|^2 = \sum_{n+1}^{t} \| z_i - \mathcal{S}_{i-1}' \phi \|^2$$

The lower index starts at n + 1 because we assume that there is no a priori information available; consequently, the first completed equation is obtained only after the n + 1th measurements. To solve this problem, we proceed as follows: Take the first n equations given by Equation 4.41, then the performance index is

$$J = \sum_{n+1}^{2n} \| z_i - \mathcal{S}_{i-1}' \phi \|^2 = \left\| \begin{bmatrix} z_{n+1} \\ \vdots \\ z_{2n} \end{bmatrix} - \begin{bmatrix} \mathcal{S}_n' \\ \vdots \\ \mathcal{S}_{2n-1}' \end{bmatrix} \phi \right\|^2$$

$$\equiv \| \mathcal{S}_{2n} - S_{2n-1} \phi \|^2$$

The solution is given by setting $\nabla_\phi J = 0$. Therefore,

$$\nabla_\phi J = -2[\mathcal{S}_{2n} - S_{2n-1}\phi]' S_{2n-1} = 0$$

Hence the solution is

$$\hat{\phi} = [S_{2n-1}' S_{2n-1}]^{-1} S_{2n-1}' \mathcal{S}_{2n} \tag{4.43}$$

Let

$$P_{2n} \triangleq [S_{2n-1}' S_{2n-1}]^{-1} \tag{4.44}$$

Hence our solution becomes

$$\hat{\phi}_{2n} = P_{2n}[S_{2n-1}]' \mathcal{S}_{2n} \tag{4.45}$$

We introduce the subscript 2n to denote the optimal estimate after the first 2n measurements. Now we will add a new measurement z_{2n+1}; the equation becomes

$$\begin{bmatrix} \mathcal{S}_{2n} \\ \hline z_{2n+1} \end{bmatrix} = \begin{bmatrix} S_{2n-1} \\ \hline \mathcal{S}_{2n}' \end{bmatrix} \phi$$

Following the same procedure, we obtain the solution

$$\hat{\phi}_{2n+1} = P_{2n+1} \left[S_{2n-1}' \;\vdots\; \mathcal{S}_{2n} \right] \begin{bmatrix} \mathcal{S}_{2n} \\ \hline z_{2n+1} \end{bmatrix} \tag{4.46}$$

where

$$P_{2n+1} \triangleq \left\{ \left[S_{2n-1}' \;\vdots\; \mathcal{S}_{2n} \right] \begin{bmatrix} S_{2n-1} \\ \hline \mathcal{S}_{2n}' \end{bmatrix} \right\}^{-1}$$

$$= \left\{ S_{2n-1}' S_{2n-1} + \mathcal{S}_{2n} \mathcal{S}_{2n}' \right\}^{-1} \equiv [P_{2n}^{-1} + \mathcal{S}_{2n} \mathcal{S}_{2n}']^{-1} \tag{4.47}$$

Using the matrix inversion lemma, we have

$$P_{2n+1} = [P_{2n}^{-1} + \mathcal{S}_{2n} \mathcal{S}_{2n}']^{-1}$$

$$= P_{2n} - P_{2n} \mathcal{S}_{2n} [\mathcal{S}_{2n}' P_{2n} \mathcal{S}_{2n} + 1]^{-1} \mathcal{S}_{2n}' P_{2n} \tag{4.48}$$

Substituting Equation 4.48 into Equation 4.46, we have

$$\hat{\phi}_{2n+1} = P_{2n+1} [S_{2n-1}' \mathcal{S}_{2n} + \mathcal{S}_{2n} z_{2n+1}]$$

$$= \hat{\phi}_{2n} - P_{2n} \mathcal{S}_{2n} [\mathcal{S}_{2n}' P_{2n} \mathcal{S}_{2n} + 1]^{-1} \mathcal{S}_{2n}' \hat{\phi}_{2n}$$

$$+ P_{2n}\mathcal{S}_{2n} z_{2n+1} - P_{2n}\mathcal{S}_{2n}[\mathcal{S}_{2n}' P_{2n}\mathcal{S}_{2n} + 1]^{-1}$$

$$\mathcal{S}_{2n}' P_{2n}\mathcal{S}_{2n} z_{2n+1}$$

$$- P_{2n}\mathcal{S}_{2n}[\mathcal{S}_{2n}' P_{2n}\mathcal{S}_{2n} + 1]^{-1} z_{2n+1}$$

$$+ P_{2n}\mathcal{S}_{2n}[\mathcal{S}_{2n}' P_{2n}\mathcal{S}_{2n} + 1]^{-1} z_{2n+1}$$

$$= \hat{\phi}_{2n} + P_{2n}\mathcal{S}_{2n}[\mathcal{S}_{2n}' P_{2n}\mathcal{S}_{2n} + 1]^{-1}[z_{2n+1} - \mathcal{S}_{2n}'\hat{\phi}_{2n}] \tag{4.49}$$

Repeating the same procedure for 2n + 2, 2n + 3, ···, we obtain the general recursive formula,

$$\hat{\phi}_{t+1} = \hat{\phi}_t + P_t\mathcal{S}_t(\mathcal{S}_t' P_t\mathcal{S}_t + 1)^{-1}(z_{t+1} - \mathcal{S}_t'\hat{\phi}_t) \tag{4.50}$$

$$P_t = P_{t-1} - P_{t-1}\mathcal{S}_{t-1}(\mathcal{S}_{t-1}' P_{t-1}\mathcal{S}_{t-1} + 1)^{-1}\mathcal{S}_{t-1}' P_{t-1} \tag{4.51}$$

For all $t \geq 2n$, starting with

$$P_{2n} = [S_{2n-1}' S_{2n-1}]^{-1}$$

$$= S_{2n-1}^{-1} S_{2n-1}'^{-1}$$

$$= [S_{2n-1}^{-1}]^2 \tag{4.52}$$

since S_{2n-1} is symmetric.

Note that the earlier equations are derived based on a set of measurement data and no a priori information is needed. Furthermore, the solution is optimal in the least-squares sense. These equations require no further matrix inversion once P_{2n} is obtained; hence these recursive relationships can be easily computed and updated in real time. In actual practice, P_{2n} need not be computed directly by matrix inversion; we can obtain it approximately by means of a mathematical trick: We shall initiate the computation process after the first n + 1 measurements by assuming $\hat{\phi}_n{}^* = 0$ and

$$P_n{}^* = \begin{bmatrix} a^2 & & & \\ & a^2 & & \\ & & \ddots & \\ & & & a^2 \end{bmatrix} = a^2 I$$

where a is very large. The recursive formula shown in Equations 4.50 and 4.51, will be used. It will be shown that after 2n measurements the solution obtained in this manner approaches the true solution as $a \to \infty$. This fact is demonstrated as follows: (The starred quantities represent the approximated solution.) The introduction of P^*_n and $\hat{\phi}^*_n$ implies the addition of a set of n equations, near trivial,

$$A\phi = z^*_n$$

$$A = \frac{1}{a}[I]$$

$$z^*_n = \begin{bmatrix} \epsilon \\ \epsilon \\ \vdots \\ \epsilon \end{bmatrix} \qquad p^*_n = a^2 I$$

where ϵ is very small and a is very large. From Equation 4.44, we have

$$P^*_n = [A'A]^{-1} = \begin{bmatrix} a^2 & & & \\ & a^2 & & \\ & & \ddots & \\ & & & a^2 \end{bmatrix}$$

Using Equation 4.45, we have

$$\hat{\phi}^*_n = P^*_n A' z^*_n = \begin{bmatrix} a & & & \\ & a & & \\ & & \ddots & \\ & & & a \end{bmatrix} \begin{bmatrix} \epsilon \\ \epsilon \\ \vdots \\ \epsilon \end{bmatrix} = \begin{bmatrix} \delta \\ \delta \\ \vdots \\ \delta \end{bmatrix} \tag{4.53}$$

where $\delta \triangleq a\epsilon$.

Now, after the first n + 1 measurements, we have the additional equation

$$z_{n+1} = [\mathscr{A}_n'][\phi]$$

Using Equations 4.46 and 4.47, we have

$$\hat{\phi}_{n+1}^{*} = P_{n+1}^{*}[A'z_n^{*} + \mathscr{S}_n z_{n+1}]$$

$$= P_{n+1}^{*}\left\{\left[\frac{\epsilon}{a}\right] + \mathscr{S}_n z_{n+1}\right\} \qquad \left[\frac{\epsilon}{a}\right] \triangleq \begin{bmatrix} \frac{\epsilon}{a} \\ \frac{\epsilon}{a} \\ \vdots \\ \frac{\epsilon}{a} \end{bmatrix}$$

$$P_{n+1}^{*} \triangleq [P_n^{*-1} + \mathscr{S}_n \mathscr{S}_n']^{-1}$$

Adding still another equation, we have

$$\hat{\phi}_{n+2}^{*} = P_{n+2}^{*}\left\{\left[\frac{\epsilon}{a}\right] + \mathscr{S}_n z_{n+1} + \mathscr{S}_{n+1} z_{n+2}\right\}$$

$$P_{n+2}^{*} = [P_{n+1}^{*-1} + \mathscr{S}_{n+1}\mathscr{S}_{n+1}']^{-1}$$

$$= [P_n^{*-1} + \mathscr{S}_n\mathscr{S}_n' + \mathscr{S}_{n+1}\mathscr{S}_{n+1}']^{-1}$$

Continuing in this manner up to the $2n^{\text{th}}$ measurement, we have

$$\hat{\phi}_{2n}^{*} = P_{2n}^{*}\left\{\left[\frac{\epsilon}{a}\right] + \mathscr{S}_n z_{n+1} + \mathscr{S}_{n+1} z_{n+2} + \cdots + \mathscr{S}_{2n-1} z_{2n}\right\}$$

$$= P_{2n}^{*}\left\{\left[\frac{\epsilon}{a}\right] + S_{2n-1}' \mathscr{S}_{2n}\right\}$$

$$P_{2n}^{*} = [P_{2n-1}^{*-1} + \mathscr{S}_{2n-1}'\mathscr{S}_{2n-1}]^{-1}$$

$$\equiv [P_n^{*-1} + S_{2n-1}' S_{2n-1}]^{-1}$$

in the limit as $\epsilon \to 0$, $a \to \infty$

$$P_n^{*} \to [0]$$

$$P_{2n}^{*} \to [S_{2n-1} S_{2n-1}']^{-1} \equiv P_{2n}$$

$$\hat{\phi}_{2n}^{*} = P_{2n}^{*}\left\{\left[\frac{\epsilon}{a}\right] + S_{2n-1}' \mathscr{S}_{2n}\right\} \to P_{2n}[S_{2n-1}' \mathscr{S}_{2n}] \equiv \hat{\phi}_{2n}$$

Hence, the solution $\hat{\phi}_{2n}^*$ and subsequent solutions will be near optimal, if P_n^* is sufficiently large. For most practical purposes, near optimal is "good enough" as long as it converges. This procedure has considerable merit, since it uses a simple computational algorithm that involves only matrix multiplication and addition; no matrix inversions are necessary.

General case — the vector b has dimension m, m ≤ n. We shall consider the case where the vector b has dimension m, m ≤ n. To give a frequency domain interpretation, this is equivalent to the case where the zeros of the z-transfer function are not all at the origin. Now our difference equation becomes

$$z_{t+1} = \mathscr{S}_t{}'\phi + n_t{}'b \tag{4.54}$$

$$\mathscr{S}_t = \begin{bmatrix} z_{t-n+1} \\ \vdots \\ z_t \end{bmatrix} \qquad n_t = \begin{bmatrix} w_{t-m+1} \\ \vdots \\ w_t \end{bmatrix}$$

Since the noise w_t cannot be measured and b is in general unknown we can write an equivalent single-noise element

$$\Omega_t \triangleq n_t{}'b \tag{4.55}$$

where Ω_t is a scalar.

Therefore, we have

$$z_{t+1} = \mathscr{S}_t{}'\phi + \Omega_t \tag{4.56}$$

This equation is very similar to Equation 4.40. The only difference is that Ω_t now is correlated.

$$\begin{aligned} \Omega_t &= b_1 w_t + b_2 w_{t-1} + \cdots + b_m w_{t-m+1} \\ \Omega_{t+1} &= b_1 w_{t+1} + b_2 w_t + \cdots + b_m w_{t-m} \\ &\vdots \\ \Omega_{t+m-1} &= b_1 w_{t+m-1} + b_2 w_{t+m-2} + \cdots + b_m w_t \\ \Omega_{t+m} &= b_1 w_{t+m} + b_2 w_{t+m-1} + \cdots + b_m w_{t+1} \end{aligned} \tag{4.57}$$

From Equation 4.57, it is apparent that Ω_t is correlated with Ω_{t+1},

$\Omega_{t+2}, \cdots, \Omega_{t+m-1}$; however, it is independent with respect to Ω_{t+m}. In other words, if we take Ω_t every m samples, that is, $\Omega_t, \Omega_{t+m}, \Omega_{t+2m}, \cdots, \Omega_{t+im}$, we will have a white random sequence with zero mean. (Since w_t is assumed to be white and with zero mean.) Consequently, the technique developed in the last section will apply if we update our equations every m samples; namely,

$$\begin{bmatrix} z_{t+1} \\ z_{t+m+1} \\ \vdots \\ z_{t+im+1} \end{bmatrix} = \begin{bmatrix} \mathcal{S}_t' \\ \mathcal{S}_{t+m}' \\ \vdots \\ \mathcal{S}_{t+im}' \end{bmatrix} \phi + \begin{bmatrix} \Omega_t \\ \Omega_{t+m} \\ \vdots \\ \Omega_{t+im} \end{bmatrix} \tag{4.58}$$

The least-squares fit recursive relation is given by

$$\hat{\phi}_{(i+1)m} = \hat{\phi}_{im} + P_{im}\mathcal{S}_{im}(\mathcal{S}_{im}'P_{im}\mathcal{S}_{im} + 1)^{-1}[z_{im+1} - \mathcal{S}_{im}'\hat{\phi}_{im}]$$

$$P_{(i+1)m} = P_{im} - P_{im}\mathcal{S}_{im}(\mathcal{S}_{im}'P_{im}\mathcal{S}_{im} + 1)^{-1}\mathcal{S}_{im}'P_{im} \tag{4.59}$$

where m = const and i = 0, 1, 2, $\cdots$.

4.3.2 Identification with Both Noise and Control Inputs. In this section, we deal with the problem of identification when there are control inputs present. We assume that these inputs can be measured. We assume the model of the dynamic system to be as follows:

$$x_{t+1} = \Phi x_t + \Gamma w_t + du_t$$

$$z_t = h' x_t \tag{4.60}$$

where d, Γ, h are n $\times$ 1 vectors and z_t, u_t are measureable, and w_t is assumed to be white Gaussian random noise sequence with zero mean and finite variance.

Problem: Given the measurements, obtain the best estimate of Φ, d to within a linear transformation.

Solution: We proceed in a manner analogous to that of Section 4.3.1. Using the standard transformations mentioned previously, we can transform the system into a set of equivalent difference equations

$$z_t + a_1 z_{t-1} + \cdots + a_n z_{t-n} = b_1 w_{t-1} + b_2 w_{t-2} + \cdots$$

$$+ c_1 u_{t-1} + c_2 u_{t-2} + \cdots + c_n u_{t-n} \tag{4.61}$$

Putting it into vector form, we have

$$z_t = \mathscr{S}_{t-1}{}' \phi + n_{t-1}{}' b + B_{t-1} c \tag{4.62}$$

where

$$B_{t-1} \triangleq \begin{bmatrix} u_{t-n} \\ u_{t-n+1} \\ \vdots \\ u_{t-1} \end{bmatrix} \qquad c \triangleq \begin{bmatrix} c_n \\ c_{n-1} \\ \vdots \\ c_1 \end{bmatrix}$$

This is equivalent to

$$z_t = \mathscr{S}_{t-1}{}^{*\prime} \phi^* + n_{t-1}{}' b \tag{4.63}$$

where

$$\mathscr{S}_{t-1}{}^{*\prime} = \begin{bmatrix} z_{t-n} \\ \vdots \\ z_{t-1} \\ \hline u_{t-n} \\ \vdots \\ u_{t-1} \end{bmatrix} \qquad \phi^* = \begin{bmatrix} -a_n \\ -a_{n-1} \\ \vdots \\ -a_1 \\ \hline c_n \\ c_{n-1} \\ \vdots \\ c_1 \end{bmatrix}$$

This equation is the same as Equation 4.46, hence the solution is the same as that of the previous section (see Equations 4.50 and 4.59). Namely,

$$\hat{\phi}_{(i+1)m}{}^* = \hat{\phi}_{im}{}^* + P_{im} \mathscr{S}_{im}{}^* (\mathscr{S}_{im}{}^{*\prime} P_{im} \mathscr{S}_{im}{}^* + 1)^{-1} (z_{im+1} - \mathscr{S}_{im}{}^{*\prime} \hat{\phi}_{im}{}^*) \tag{4.64}$$

$$P_{(i+1)m} = P_{im} - P_{im} \mathscr{S}_{im}{}^* (\mathscr{S}_{im}{}^{*\prime} P_{im} \mathscr{S}_{im}{}^* + 1)^{-1} \mathscr{S}_{im}{}^{*\prime} P_{im} \tag{4.65}$$

where m is a constant choosen to assure that the effective noise input $b'w_t$ at each step is uncorrelated.

4.3.3 Process Identification When Subjected to Noise With Unknown Mean. Consider the case now when w_t has a nonzero mean, say $\overline{w}$, Equation 4.63 becomes

$$z_t = \mathcal{S}_{t-1}^{*'}\phi^* + n_{t-1}'b$$

$$\triangleq \mathcal{S}_{t-1}^{*'}\phi^* + \Omega_{t-1}^{*} + \overline{\Omega} \qquad (4.66)$$

where Ω_{t-1} is an equivalent correlated noise with zero mean, $\overline{\Omega}$ is the mean of $n_{t-1}'b$.

Two alternate solutions are possible for this case.

1. We can rewrite Equation 4.66 in the following form:

$$z_t = \mathcal{S}_{t-1}^{**'}\phi^{**} + \Omega_{t-1}^{*} \qquad (4.67)$$

where

$$\mathcal{S}_{t-1}^{**} = \begin{bmatrix} z_{t-n} \\ \vdots \\ z_{t-1} \\ \hline n_{t-n} \\ \vdots \\ n_{t-1} \\ \hline 1 \end{bmatrix} \qquad \phi^{**} = \begin{bmatrix} -a_n \\ -a_{n-1} \\ \vdots \\ -a_1 \\ \hline c_n \\ \vdots \\ c_1 \\ \hline \overline{\Omega} \end{bmatrix}$$

Equation 4.67 is in the same form, as Equations 4.56 and 4.63; therefore the results of Equations 4.64 and 4.65 apply; namely,

$$\hat{\phi}^{**}_{(i+1)m} = \hat{\phi}^{**}_{im} + P_{im}\mathcal{S}^{**}_{im}(\mathcal{S}^{**'}_{im}P_{im}\mathcal{S}^{**}_{im} + 1)^{-1}(z_{im+1} - \mathcal{S}^{**'}_{im}\hat{\phi}_{im})$$

$$P_{(i+1)m} = P_{im} - P_{im}\mathcal{S}^{**}_{im}(\mathcal{S}^{**'}_{im}P_{im}\mathcal{S}^{**}_{im} + 1)^{-1}\mathcal{S}^{**'}_{im}P_{im} \qquad (4.68)$$

2. If we do not wish to estimate the unknown mean, we can proceed as follows. Define

$$z_t^* \triangleq z_t - z_{t-1}$$

Therefore,

$$\begin{aligned} z_t^* &= z_t - z_{t-1} \\ &= \mathcal{S}^{*\prime}_{t-1}\phi^* - \mathcal{S}^{*\prime}_{t-2}\phi^* + \Omega^*_{t-1} - \Omega^*_{t-2} \end{aligned}$$

Hence we can rewrite Equation 4.66 into the following form:

$$\begin{aligned} z_t^* &= \mathcal{S}^{**\prime}_{t-1}\phi^* + \Omega^{**}_{t-1} \\ \Omega^{**}_{t-1} &\triangleq \Omega^*_{t-1} - \Omega^*_{t-2} \end{aligned} \tag{4.69}$$

where Ω^{**}_{t-1} is a correlated noise with zero mean, and

$$\mathcal{S}^{**}_{t-1} = \begin{bmatrix} z^*_{t-n} \\ \vdots \\ z^*_{t-1} \\ \hline u^*_{t-n} \\ \vdots \\ u^*_{t-1} \end{bmatrix} \qquad \phi^* = \begin{bmatrix} -a_n \\ -a_{n-1} \\ \vdots \\ -a_1 \\ \hline c_n \\ \vdots \\ c_1 \end{bmatrix}$$

$$u_t^* \triangleq u_t - u_{t-1}$$

Equation 4.67 is in the same form, as Equations 4.56 and 4.63, therefore the results of Equations 4.64 and 4.65 apply; namely,

$$\hat{\phi}^*_{(i+1)m} = \hat{\phi}^*_{im} + P_{im}\mathcal{S}^{**}_{im}(\mathcal{S}^{**\prime}_{im}P_{im}\mathcal{S}^{**}_{im} + 1)^{-1}(z^*_{im+1} - \mathcal{S}^{**\prime}_{im}\hat{\phi}^*_{im})$$

$$P_{(i+1)m} = P_{im} - P_{im}\mathcal{S}^{**}_{im}(\mathcal{S}^{**\prime}_{im}P_{im}\mathcal{S}^{**}_{im} + 1)^{-1}\mathcal{S}^{**\prime}_{im}P_{im} \tag{4.70}$$

4.3.4 Process Identification When Subjected to Correlated Noise. In the theoretical developments thus far, white noise had been assumed. The results obtained can readily be extended to the case where the noise is correlated. If the noise is of rational spectrum, it is common knowledge that it could be represented by a white noise passing through a linear filter. As a consequence, we can enlarge the parametric state space to include this linear filter; hence, the extension is trivial. For practical purposes, the technique of waiting m samples before up-dating, discussed in the general case, is often to be preferred. Although the techniques presented there may appear extravagant, however they do offer the following advantages:

1. It eliminates the identification of vector b. (In general, the vector b is not identifiable without measuring the noise input.)
2. If the noise is correlated with power spectrum of unknown order, this procedure eliminates its consideration as long as its significant correlation interval is less than m sample period where m is now determined by the order of vector b plus the interval of significant correlation.
3. It also eliminates the additional complication of an enlarged parametric state space; this advantage is especially pronounced when the system is subjected to control inputs.

4.4. Parameter Tracking for Nonstationary Systems

Now, we will consider the case where the system parameter ϕ changes with time. First of all, let us consider the following case:

4.4.1 Parameter Variations Describable by a Linear Dynamic Process. Now we will consider that the parameters vary according to the following dynamic relationship:

$$\phi_{t+1} = \Psi\phi_t \tag{4.71}$$

where Ψ is a known transition matrix. Putting Equation 4.40 together with Equation 4.71, we have a relationship identical to that of Equation 3.49. Using the methods of least-squares with a dynamic interpretation discussed in Section 3.4.2, we have

$$\begin{aligned} \hat{\phi}_{t+1} &= \Psi\phi_t + M_{t+1}\mathcal{S}_t(\mathcal{S}_t' M_{t+1}\mathcal{S}_t + 1)^{-1}[z_{t+1} - \mathcal{S}_t' \hat{\phi}_t] \\ M_{t+1} &= \Psi P_t \Psi' \\ P_{t+1} &= M_{t+1} - M_{t+1}\mathcal{S}_t(\mathcal{S}_t' M_{t+1}\mathcal{S}_t + 1)^{-1}\mathcal{S}_t' M_{t+1} \end{aligned} \tag{4.72}$$

Now if we further perturb the parameter variations with a random noise, say by adding a term $\beta\alpha_t$ to Equation 4.71, where β is a known vector and α_t is a white Gaussian noise with zero mean and variance σ^2, we may extrapolate Equation 4.72 by brute force and obtain the following relationships:

$$\hat{\phi}_{t+1} = \Psi\hat{\phi}_t + M_{t+1}\mathcal{S}_t(\mathcal{S}_t' M_{t+1}\mathcal{S}_t + 1)^{-1}[z_{t+1} - \mathcal{S}_t'\Psi\hat{\phi}_t]$$

$$M_{t+1} = \Psi P_t \Psi' + A$$
$$P_{t+1} = M_{t+1} - M_{t+1}(\mathscr{S}_t' M_{t+1} \mathscr{S}_t + 1)^{-1} \mathscr{S}_t' M_{t+1} \tag{4.73}$$

where A is a constant matrix choosen by experimentation. Note that the scheme presented in Equation 4.72 is still optimal in a deterministic sense whereas that of Equation 4.73 is no longer optimal in any sense, the only justification is that "it works," as will be demonstrated later in the experiments.

4.4.2 Parameter Variation of Unknown Nature — Nonoptimal Tracking. Here we will consider the case where we know the parameter varies with time, but we do not know the exact relationship that governs their variations, for example, Ψ is not know It is desired to have the identifier exhibit some tracking behavior. Since Ψ is unknown, we can assume that $\Psi = (I)$ and we will arbitrarily raise the constant matrix A in Equation 4.73. This gives a physical interpretation that our parameter variation is rather random and with large deviations. In the computation process, m_t in the limit will approach a constant matrix from above; hence, the weighting term for the residue will not go to zero, and the estimation scheme will always tend to track the actual trend of the variations. It is important to note here that this procedure is purely intuitive and has no assurance of convergence. Its usefulness in practice must be determined by experimentation with the particular systems involved.

4.4.3 An Alternate Procedure. If it is known that the parameters vary relatively slowly in comparison to the convergence rate of the identification process, an alternate procedure may be used. Here, we neglect Ψ and α, and simply apply the least-squares fit procedure for finite data as discussed in the special case. The identification process is computed according to Equations 4.50 and 4.51 starting with an initial estimate $\hat{\phi}_0, P_0$. If we know from previous experience that the identification process converges to within an acceptable limit in k iterations, then we can reinitiate the identification process every k iterations, starting with the last estimate $\hat{\phi}_m$ and the same P_0. This type of procedure artificially places more weight on the current data, hence, we may expect the current estimate to track the trend of the slow parameter variations closely. Again, it must be emphasized that the procedures are intuitive extensions of the optimal identification process and are without rigorous theoretical foundation.

4.5 Stochastic Interpretation

As mentioned previously, the computational scheme developed thus far is purely deterministic. It can be applied to any set of equations and obtain the least-squares fit solution without regard to how these equations come about. However, if we wish to consider the statistical properties of the estimate, that is, consistency, and so forth, we must take into consideration how these equations come about, how and where the noise enters into the system, and what statistical characteristics it has. In this section, we shall attempt to give some stochastic justification to our scheme. To begin with, we shall discuss the following:

4.5.1 The Relationships with the Kalman Filter. Throughout this chapter, we have discussed the least-squares fit solution to a set of linear equations

$$z = \begin{bmatrix} z_1 \\ z_2 \\ \vdots \\ z_\ell \end{bmatrix} = \begin{bmatrix} \mathcal{S}_0' \\ \mathcal{S}_1' \\ \vdots \\ \mathcal{S}_{\ell-1}' \end{bmatrix} \phi + \begin{bmatrix} w_0 \\ w_1 \\ \vdots \\ w_{\ell-1} \end{bmatrix} \equiv A_\ell \phi + n_\ell \quad (4.74)$$

where $\ell \geq n$, A is $n \times \ell$, n is the order of ϕ, and w_t is white with zero mean and variance σ^2. As shown in the previous section, the least-squares fit solution is given by

$$\hat{\phi}_\ell = (A_\ell' A_\ell)^{-1} A_\ell' z$$

$$\triangleq P_\ell A_\ell' z \quad (4.75)$$

Equation 4.75 can in turn be put into a recursive relation shown in Equation 4.50. If the matrix A is deterministic and the noise is Gaussian, we have shown in Chapter 3 that this result is identical to that of the Kalman filter. Hence, the solution possesses all the "nice" properties of the Kalman filter. Unfortunately, in this case, the elements of the A_ℓ's are made up of past outputs; consequently, they are not deterministic. This is further complicated by the fact that the system outputs are correlated with all the past w_s's. Consequently, the problem becomes considerably more complicated. However, if we can make A_ℓ's independent with the vector n_ℓ, we can once again prove consistency. In what follows, we shall assume that the system we are identifying is stable and that each output will have significant correlation only with the finite past. Then if we take data far enough apart in time such that each new equation is essentially independent of the past noise w's. Thus, we have assured that A_ℓ is independent of n_ℓ. Then, combining Equations 4.74 and 4.75 and rearranging, we have

$$\phi - \hat{\phi}_\ell = (A'A)^{-1} A'(-n_\ell) \quad (4.76)$$

The expected value is

$$E = [\hat{\phi}_\ell - \phi] = E[(A'A)^{-1}A'(+n_\ell)]$$

$$= E[(A'A)^{-1}A']E[n_\ell]$$

$$= 0 \tag{4.77}$$

Hence, the estimate is unbiased.

The covariance matrix is

$$E[(\phi - \hat{\phi}_\ell)(\phi - \hat{\phi}_\ell)'] \triangleq \tilde{P}_\ell$$

$$= E[(A_\ell'A_\ell)^{-1}A_\ell'n_\ell n_\ell'A_\ell(A_\ell'A_\ell)^{-1}]$$

$$= E[(A_\ell'A_\ell)^{-1}A_\ell'E(n_\ell n_\ell')A_\ell(A_\ell'A_\ell)^{-1}]$$

$$= E[(A_\ell' A_\ell)^{-1}A_\ell'[Q]A_\ell(A_\ell'A_\ell)^{-1}] \tag{4.78}$$

If w_t is white, with variance σ^2 and zero mean, we have

$$Q = \sigma^2[I]$$

Substituting into Equation 4.78, we have

$$\tilde{P}_\ell = E[(A_\ell'A_\ell)^{-1}A_\ell'\sigma^2[I]A_\ell(A_\ell'A_\ell)^{-1}]$$

$$= E[\sigma^2(A_\ell'A_\ell)^{-1}A_\ell'A_\ell(A_\ell'A_\ell)^{-1}]$$

$$= E[\sigma^2(A_\ell'A_\ell)^{-1}]$$

$$\triangleq \sigma^2\overline{P}_\ell \tag{4.79}$$

where

$$\overline{P}_\ell \triangleq (\overline{A_\ell'A_\ell})^{-1}$$

Equation 4.79 states that the mean of P_ℓ is directly related to the covariance matrix, hence in each identification process, $\sigma^2 P_\ell$ is an unbiased estimator of the covariance matrix $\tilde{P}_\ell$. Since P_ℓ always $\rightarrow [0]$, deterministically, as $\ell \rightarrow \infty$ and $\tilde{P}_\ell$ will also $\rightarrow [0]$.

Together with the fact that $\hat{\phi}_\ell$ is unbiased, this shows the estimate to be consistent. In other words

$$\lim_{\ell \to \infty} \hat{\phi}_\ell = \phi$$

4.5.2 Consistency of the Identification. As shown in the previous section, if the equations are taken far enough apart in time, our estimate scheme is quite similar to that of the Kalman filter. The only difference being that P is now an estimator of the covariance matrix rather than the covariance matrix itself. Unfortunately, this proof of consistency is only of theoretical interest, since in practice we cannot afford to wait "long enough" for these assumptions to hold. If we insisted on updating our estimates every sample or every few samples, the matrix A_ℓ is definitely correlated with n_ℓ and the bias becomes

$$\overline{\hat{\phi}_\ell - \phi} = E[(A_\ell' A_\ell)^{-1} A_\ell' n_\ell] \triangleq \bar{c}_\ell$$

Since A_ℓ contains linear combinations of the elements in n_ℓ, then $(A_\ell' A_\ell)^{-1} A_\ell' n_\ell$ is a vector whose elements are made up of ratios of two polynomial containing the elements of n_ℓ. The evaluation of the mean is not a simple task, especially when ℓ is large. One thing is certain, however, the bias $\bar{c}_\ell$ in general will be finite and different from zero. Consequencly, we can conclude that our estimate $\hat{\phi}_\ell$ is biased for finite ℓ. Therefore, to prove consistency we must show that the bias will approach zero as ℓ increases. This property could be as follows: Let

$$c_\ell \triangleq \hat{\phi}_\ell - \phi = (A_\ell' A_\ell)^{-1} A_\ell' n_\ell$$

Now if we add an equation, we have

$$\begin{bmatrix} z_\ell \\ --- \\ z_{\ell+1} \end{bmatrix} = \begin{bmatrix} A_\ell \\ --- \\ \mathcal{S}_\ell' \end{bmatrix} \phi + \begin{bmatrix} n_\ell \\ --- \\ w_\ell \end{bmatrix}$$

Therefore,

$$\begin{aligned} c_{\ell+1} &= (A_{\ell+1}' A_{\ell+1})^{-1} A_{\ell+1}' n_{\ell+1} \\ &= (A_\ell' A_\ell + \mathcal{S}_\ell \mathcal{S}_\ell')^{-1} [A_\ell' n_\ell + \mathcal{S}_\ell w_\ell] \\ &= (A_\ell' A_\ell + \mathcal{S}_\ell \mathcal{S}_\ell')^{-1} (A_\ell' A_\ell)\, c_\ell \\ &\quad + (A_\ell' A_\ell + \mathcal{S}_\ell \mathcal{S}_\ell')^{-1} \mathcal{S}_\ell w_\ell \end{aligned}$$

$$\triangleq \Psi_\ell^* c_\ell + \Gamma_\ell^* w_\ell$$

Note that w_ℓ is independent of Γ_ℓ^* and Ψ_ℓ^*, also Ψ_ℓ^* has eigenvalues $0 < \lambda_i < 1$ for all i. This latter property is shown as follows: Let

$$\Psi^* \triangleq [P + Q]^{-1} P$$

where $P \triangleq A_\ell' A_\ell$ = positive definite and $Q \triangleq \mathcal{S}_\ell \mathcal{S}_\ell'$ = positive semidefinite and rank 1.

To find the eigenvalues, we write

$$[P + Q]^{-1} Px = \lambda x \qquad x \triangleq \text{eigenvector of } [P + Q]^{-1} P.$$

Premultiplied by x', we have

$$x' Px = \lambda x'[P + Q]x$$

Hence,

$$[1 - \lambda] x' Px = \lambda x' Qx$$

Since P is positive definite and Q is positive semidefinite and of rank 1, the eigenvalue λ must satisfy the following condition:

$$0 < \lambda < 1$$

Consequently, we can represent this relationship as that of a stable time-varying linear system driven by white noise and with (IC) initial condition c_n. See Figure 4.5.

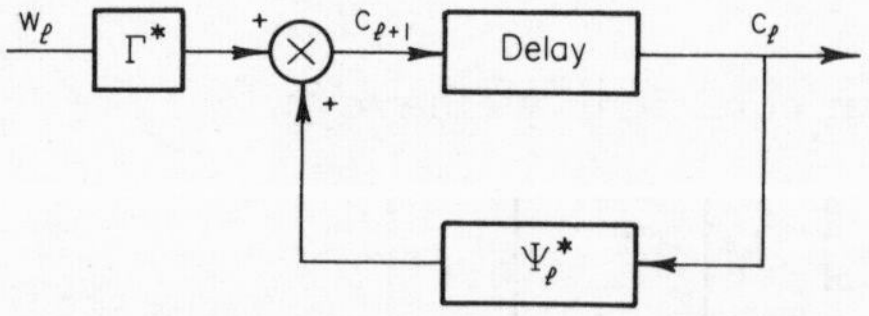

Figure 4.5. Linear system driven by white noise. ($IC = c_n \quad \ell \geq n$)

Since the system is stable for all ℓ's, it is apparent that the effect of the IC will approach 0 as $\ell \to \infty$; hence, $\overline{c_\ell} \to \overline{g_\ell^* w_\ell} \to 0$ where g_ℓ^* is some constant vector. Therefore,

$$\lim_{\ell \to \infty} \overline{(\hat{\phi}_\ell - \phi)} = \lim_{\ell \to \infty} \overline{c}_\ell = 0$$

Therefore, the identification is unbiased as $\ell \to \infty$. This, coupled with the stability of the identification process, assures consistency. This fact is demonstrated in all the computational examples shown in the next section.

4.6 Computation Results

The computational scheme generated in the previous section (Section 4.5) is programmed for digital computation. A second- and fourth-order model are used in the computational experiment, as follows:

1. Second-order model.

$$\Phi^* = \begin{bmatrix} 0 & 1 \\ -a_2 & -a_1 \end{bmatrix} \qquad \Gamma = \begin{bmatrix} 0 \\ 1 \end{bmatrix} \qquad h^* = \begin{bmatrix} 1 \\ 0 \end{bmatrix}$$

This is equivalent to an underdamped second-order sampled data system shown in Figure 4.6.

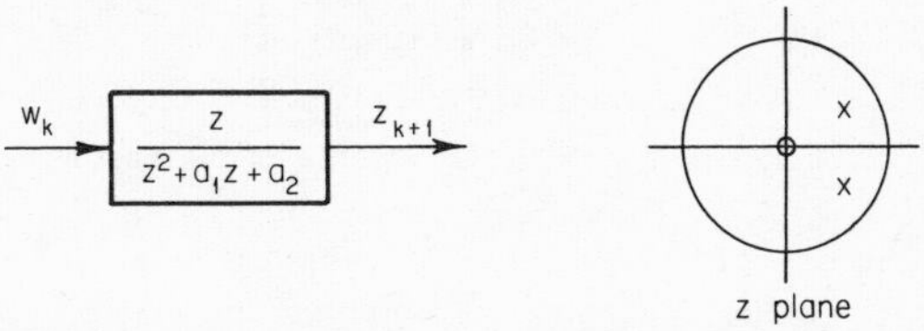

Figure 4.6. Sampled data system representation.

The eigenvalues are

$$\lambda = -\frac{a_1}{2} \pm \frac{\sqrt{a_1^2 - 4a_2}}{2}$$

2. Fourth-order model.

$$\Phi^* = \begin{bmatrix} 0 & 1 & 0 & 0 \\ 0 & 0 & 1 & 0 \\ 0 & 0 & 0 & 1 \\ -0.656 & +0.784 & -0.18 & 1.0 \end{bmatrix} \qquad \Gamma = \begin{bmatrix} 0 \\ 0 \\ 0 \\ 1 \end{bmatrix} \qquad h^* = \begin{bmatrix} 1 \\ 0 \\ 0 \\ 0 \end{bmatrix}$$

This is equivalent (see Figure 4.7) to a z-transfer function.

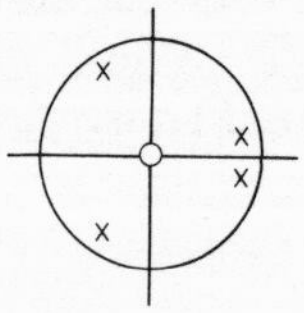

Figure 4.7. Pole zero locations in the z plane.

$$G(z) = \frac{z^3}{(z^2 - 1.8z + 0.8z)(z^2 + 0.8z + 0.8z)}$$

which has two pairs of underdamped roots. Except for the numerator, this could be considered as a hypothetical missile with the short period and the first-bending mode included.

4.6.1 Experiment I: Effect of Input Noise Level. The fourth-order model is used here. The basic equations of computational

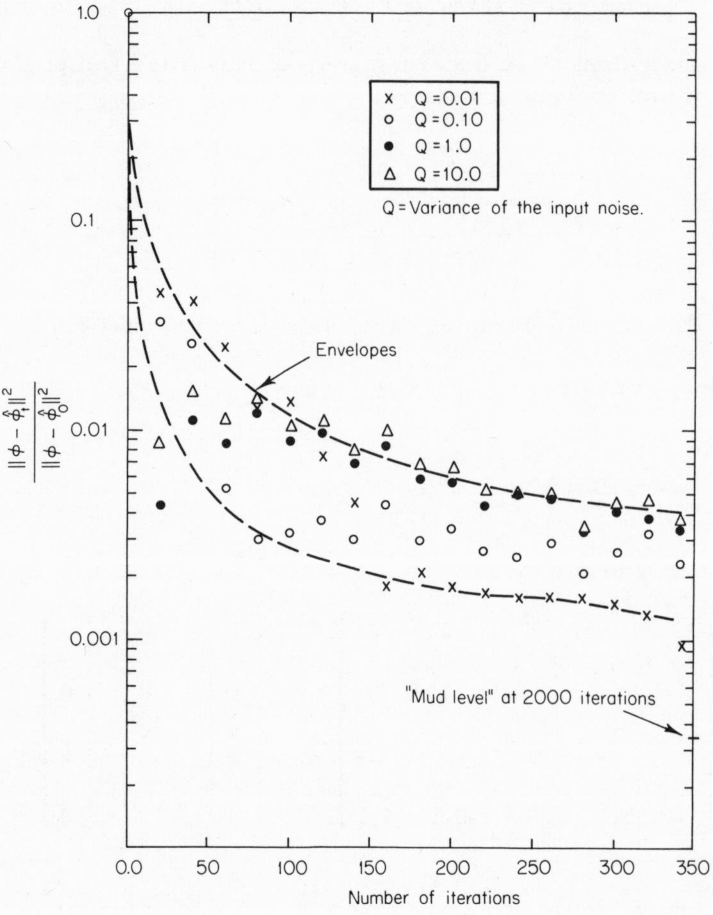

Figure 4.8. Effect of noise amplitude a upon the identification.

Program 1 (Appendix B) were used in this computation. Four different noise levels (σ^2 = 0.01, 0.1, 1.0, 10.0) were used in the experiment. In all cases, the initial estimate $\hat{\phi}_0$ is assumed to be exactly opposite to the true ϕ and the initial P_0 = 100[I]. The computational results are presented in Figure 4.8. In all cases, the estimation error converges rapidly at first until it reaches the "mud level" (below 1 percent of the original error) where it begins to slow down and asymtotically approach the true ϕ. Note that for this problem, the time constant of the slowest mode is roughly 10 samples. If we define the time to reach mud level as 3 time constants of the identifier, then from the computer results we can state that the time constant for the identification process is roughly 3 times that of the lowest significant mode. (This is just a rule of thumb.) In all cases, the identifier is working

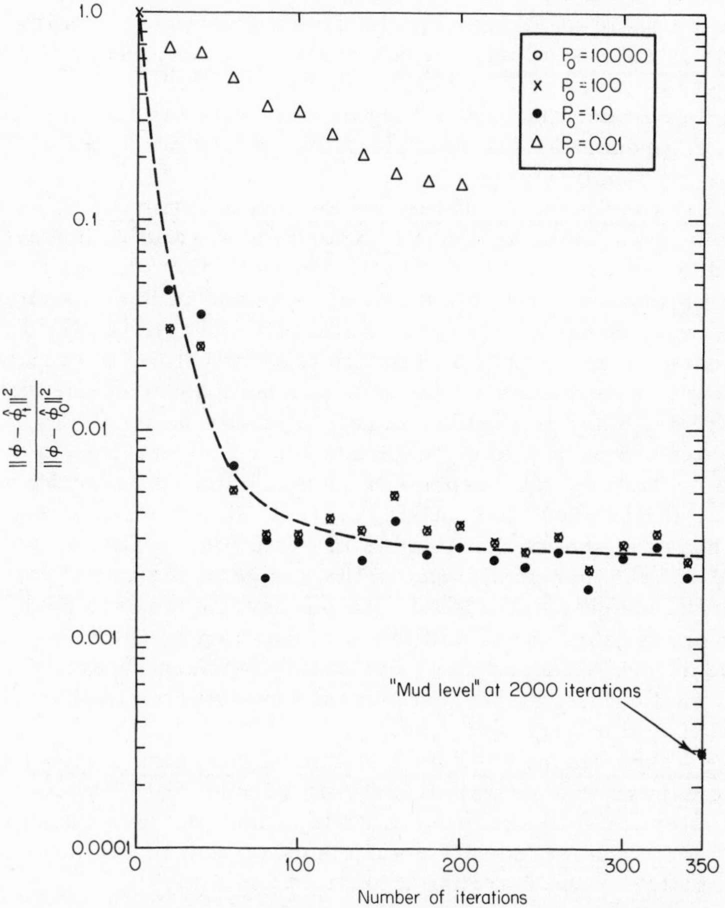

Figure 4.9. Effect of the variation of P_0 on the identification.

with signals generated purely by a noise input. The convergence properties for different noise levels are roughly the same. The mud level is higher for larger noise (variance) input as is expected.

4.6.2 Experiment 2: Effect of the Variation of P_0. The problem is exactly the same as that in Experiment 1, except that in this case we fixed the variance Q = 0.1 and vary P_0. As is shown in Section 4.3, we will have the least-squares fit solution if we let $P_0 = [\infty]$. In practice, however, we can only use finite P_0. The object of this experiment is to study the effect of P_0 on the identification. Four different $P_0 = [0.01], [1.0], [10.0], [10,000]$ were used in this experiment. Also $\hat{\phi}_0$ remains to be opposite to ϕ. The results are shown in Figure 4.9. As would be expected in the case where $P_0 = [0.01]$, the convergence is very slow, since the weighting function of the residues becomes too small and the residues can hardly affect the estimates. Note that for cases where the value of $P_0 \geq [1.0]$, the convergence of the estimation scheme is quite similar. In fact there is no noticeable difference between the cases of $P_0 = [100]$ and $P_0 = [10,000]$. These results are rather important, since they demonstrate the fact that the convergence properties are not affected significantly by P_0 as long as it is reasonably large.

4.6.3 Experiment 3: Effect of the Initial Estimate. The basic problem is the same as that of Experiments 1 and 2, however P_0 and Q are fixed at (100), (0.1), respectively. Three different initial estimates $\hat{\phi}_0 = [-\phi], [0], [\simeq \phi]$ are used in the experiment. The computational results are shown in Figure 4.10. Note that the identification results are identical for all three cases after the first few iterations. This fact was demonstrated theoretically in Section 4.3 and is verified here. It should be pointed out that in the case when $\hat{\phi}_0 \simeq \phi$ the estimate after 20 iterations is worse than $\hat{\phi}_0$. This is to be expected, since we used a large P_0 and this has the effect of essentially disregarding the initial estimate. If we have reasonable confidence in our initial estimate, then we should reflect this confidence in the choice of the initial P_0. Since P_0 can be roughly associated with the covariance (see Section 4.5) of the error, the more confidence we have on $\hat{\phi}_0$ the smaller the P_0 should be. The precise relationship between P_0 and $\hat{\phi}_0$ is not known analytically at present. It may be determined with further research and experimentation.

4.6.4 Experiment 4: Effect of Both Control and Noise Inputs. In this experiment a first-order over second-order model is used. The system is subjected to a unit step input and noise disturbance. The objective is to identify coefficients of both the numerator and denominator. The z-transfer function used is

$$G(z) = -\frac{(z + 0.5)}{z^2 - 1.8z + 0.8z}$$

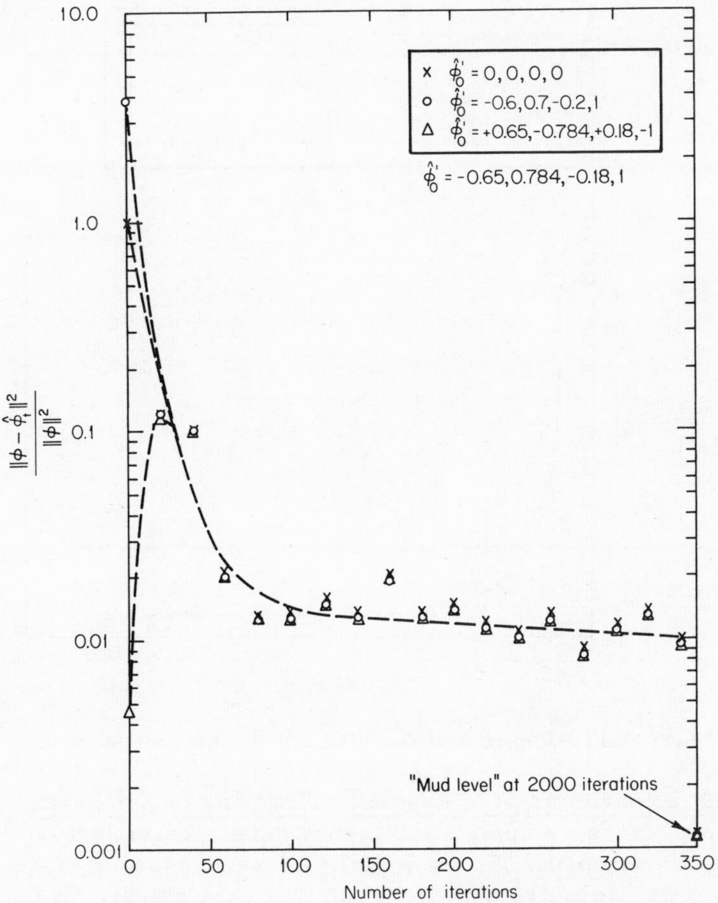

Figure 4.10. Effect of initial guess $\hat{\phi}_0$ on the identification.

$$[Q] = [0.3333] \qquad P_0 = [100]$$

$$\phi^* = \begin{bmatrix} -0.82 \\ 1.8 \\ 1.0 \\ 5 \end{bmatrix} \qquad \hat{\phi}_0^* = \begin{bmatrix} 0 \\ 0 \\ 0 \\ 0 \end{bmatrix}$$

The results are shown in Figure 4.11. The $||\hat{\phi}^* - \phi^*||^2$ converges to within 0.2 percent of $||\phi^*||^2$ in 10 iterations. Note that the computational Program 2 (Appendix B) is used for this experiment.

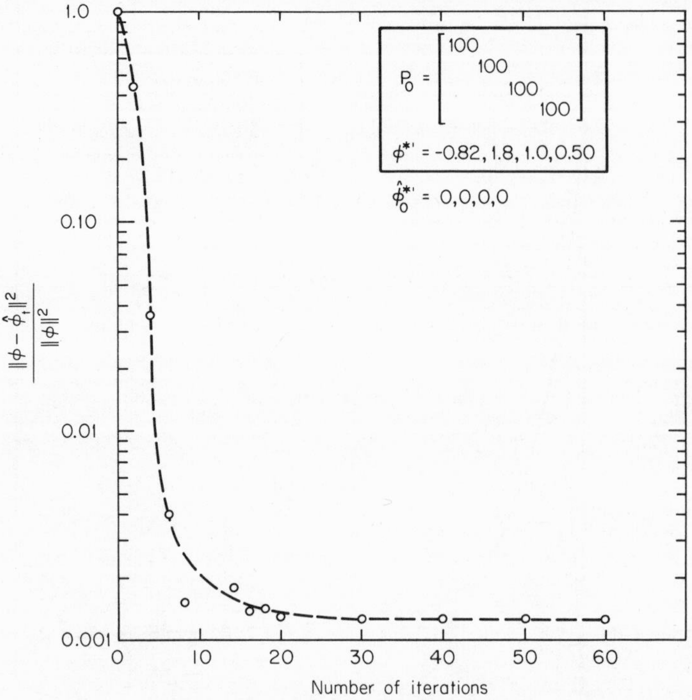

Figure 4.11. Identification with noise and unit step input.

4.6.5 Experiment 5: Parameter Tracking of Nonstationary Systems. Here we applied the theory developed in Section 4.4 into the experiment. For simplicity, a second-order system is used. Two cases are considered in this experiment. In Case 1, one system parameter is assumed to grow by 2 percent each iteration, while the other is being held constant. The trajectory of poles in the z plane is shown in Figure 4.12. Note that the system changes from a stable to an unstable system during the experiment. The computational results are shown in Figures 4.13 and 4.14. In both cases, $\hat{\phi}_0 = [-\phi]$, $P_0 = [100]$, $Q = [0.33]$ were used. The results demonstrate excellent tracking behavior. In Case 2, the basic problem is the same except that noise is added to cause further variation in the parameters. The trajectory of the poles is shown in Figure 4.15.

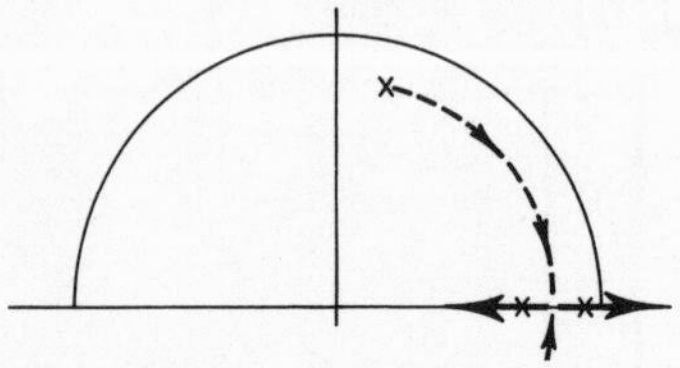

Figure 4.12. Trajectory of the poles in the z plane (Case 1).

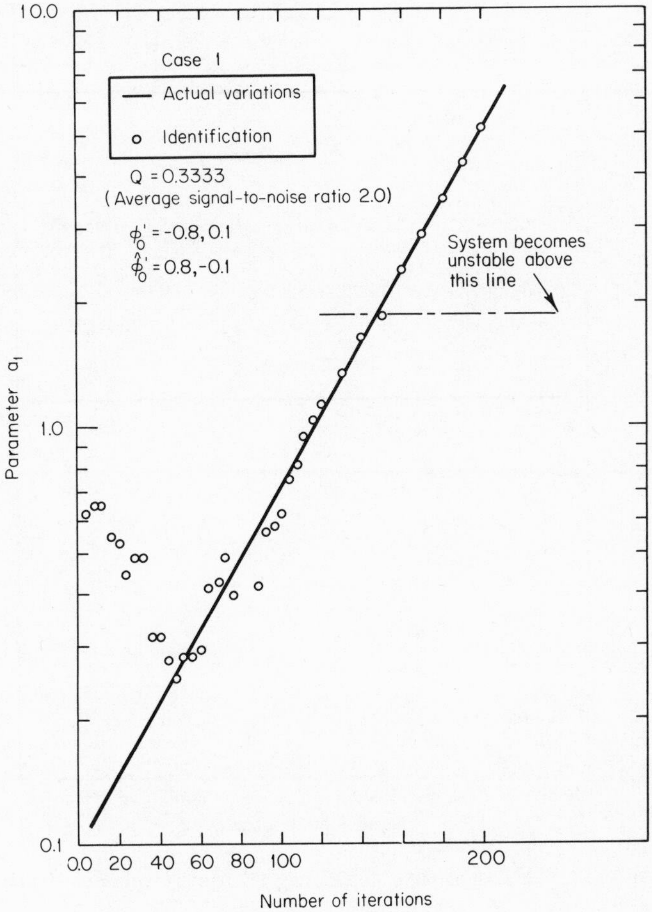

Figure 4.13. Parameter tracking (nonstationary system, second-order).

Note that the trajectory moves in the opposite direction due to the finite sampled mean of the initial noise disturbances. The computational results are shown in Figures 4.16 and 4.17. Excellent tracking behavior of the identifier was demonstrated in spite of large random variations of the parameters from sample to sample.

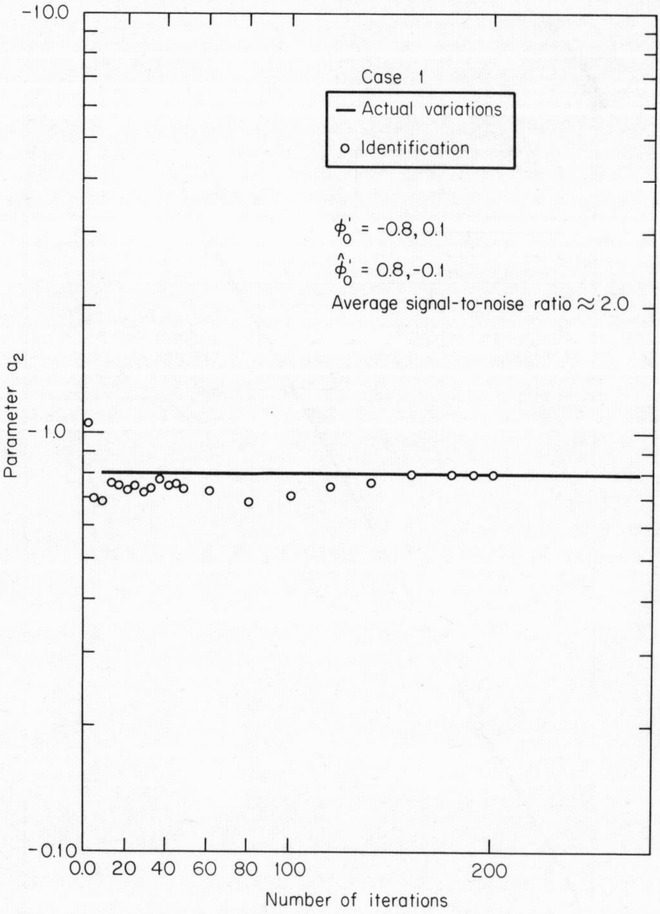

Figure 4.14. Parameter tracking (nonstationary system).

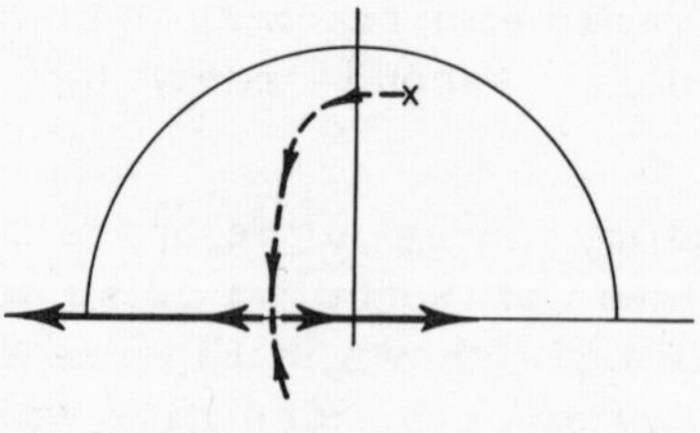

Figure 4.15. Trajectory of poles in the z plane (Case 2).

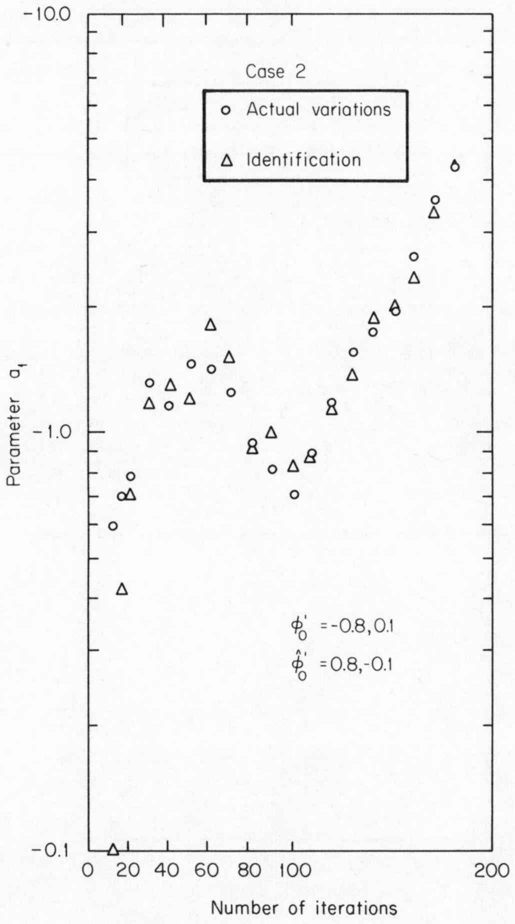

Figure 4.16. Parameter tracking (nonstationary system); parameter driven by random noise.

4.7. Summary

In this chapter, the problem of identification of linear system parameters is studied. The necessary and sufficient condition for identification is first derived for the deterministic case. This technique is then extended to cover the case where the order of the system is unknown. A computational scheme is developed for the stochastic case where the system is subjected to noise and control inputs. The method of least-squares fit over finite data is employed in this development. The resultant computational scheme is then extended to treat cases with correlated noise, noise with unknown mean, and nonstationary systems. It

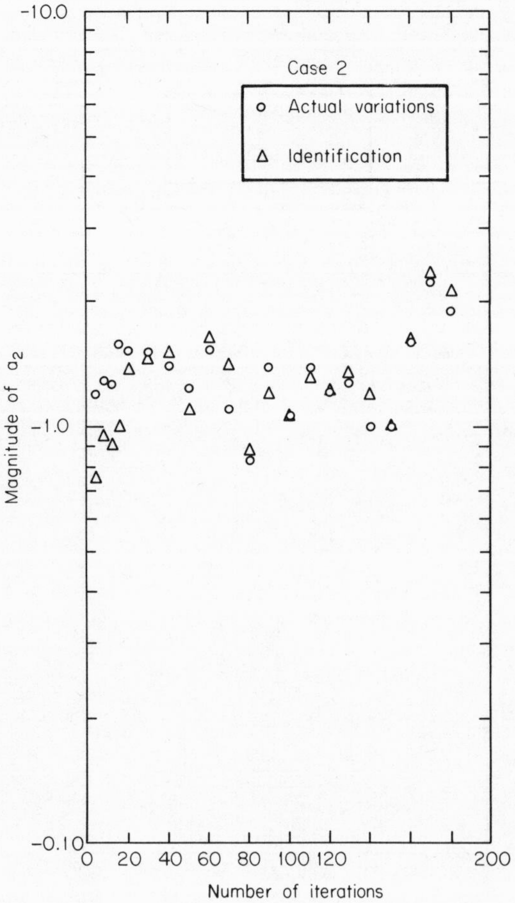

Figure 4.17. Parameter tracking; system parameter driven by random noise.

was shown that this identification scheme is consistent in that

$$\lim_{\ell \to \infty} \hat{\phi}_\ell = \phi$$

This is verified by experimental (computational) results. It is the author's opinion that this scheme offers considerable promise; it could be applied to practical systems with further investigation.

Chapter 5

OPTIMAL CLOSED-LOOP CONTROL SYSTEMS

In Chapters 2, 3, and 4, we discussed the theory of optimal estimation, identification, and control. In this chapter, we shall discuss how some of these theories could be used in practical applications. In particular, we shall derive optimal closed-loop controllers for some special classes of systems. We shall begin by considering the following:

5.1 Derivation of the Optimal Closed-Loop Control Law for Linear Deterministic Systems with Quadratic Criterion

In Chapter 2, various analytical and computational techniques for finding the optimal control law were discussed. Except for the direct computation via dynamic programming, all these techniques provide optimal control laws as a function of time, often referred to as open-loop solutions. For most control applications, it is desirable to have closed-loop solutions, where the control law is given as a function of states. Unfortunately, these closed-loop solutions are often extremely difficult to obtain. In the following, we will treat the special case of a linear system with quadratic criterion. This case is chosen because it is one of the rare cases in which closed-loop solutions can be obtained. Further, the optimal-feedback solution obtained is a linear function of the states. The simplicity of the solution and mechanization has made this class of systems of considerable practical importance. In what follows, a discrete controllable linear system with no inequality constraints is solved using calculus.† The basic problem is specified as follows:

Problem:

$$\min J = \frac{1}{2}\|x_n\|_A^2 + \sum_{i=0}^{n-1} \frac{1}{2}\|Hx_{i+1}\|_Q^2 + \frac{1}{2}\|u_i\|_R^2 \tag{5.1}$$

Subject to the constraints

† This problem had been solved by numerous other authors. Most of them employed the technique of dynamic programming to derive their results. The method of ordinary calculus is used here for its simplicity.

$$x_{i+1} = \Phi x_i + Du_i \qquad x_0 = x(0) \tag{5.2}$$

Using the method of Lagrange multipliers, we have

$$J^* \triangleq J + \sum_{i=0}^{n-1} \langle \lambda_i \cdot (x_{i+1} - \Phi x_i - Du_i) \rangle \tag{5.3}$$

Setting $\nabla_{x_i} J^*$, $\nabla_{x_i} J^*$, $\nabla_{u_i} J^* = 0$ for all i' s (except $\nabla_{x_0} J^*$ since x_0 is given, hence no free variation), we have the following set of relations:

$$\begin{cases} \dfrac{\partial J^{*\prime}}{\partial u_0} = Ru_0 - D'\lambda_0 = 0 \\ \dfrac{\partial J^{*\prime}}{\partial \lambda_0} = x_1 - \Phi x_0 - Du_0 = 0 \end{cases}$$

$$\begin{cases} \dfrac{\partial J^{*\prime}}{\partial x_1} = H'QHx_1 + \lambda_0 - \Phi'\lambda_1 = 0 \\ \dfrac{\partial J^{*\prime}}{\partial u_1} = Ru_1 - D'\lambda_1 = 0 \\ \dfrac{\partial J^{*\prime}}{\partial \lambda_1} = x_2 - \Phi x_1 - Du_1 = 0 \end{cases}$$

$$\vdots \tag{5.4}$$

$$\begin{cases} \dfrac{\partial J^{*\prime}}{\partial x_{n-1}} = H'QHx_{n-1} + \lambda_{n-2} - \Phi'\lambda_{n-1} = 0 \\ \dfrac{\partial J^{*\prime}}{\partial u_{n-1}} = Ru_{n-1} - D'\lambda_{n-1} = 0 \\ \dfrac{\partial J^{*\prime}}{\partial \lambda_{n-1}} = x_n - \Phi x_{n-1} - Du_{n-1} = 0 \end{cases}$$

$$\frac{\partial J^{*\prime}}{\partial x_n} = Ax_n + \lambda_{n-1} + H'QHx_n = 0$$

From the last two sets of equations, we have

$$\begin{aligned} \lambda_{n-1} &= -[A + H'QH]x_n \\ &\triangleq -P_0 x_n \end{aligned} \tag{5.5}$$

$$\begin{aligned} u_{n-1} &= R^{-1}D'\lambda_{n-1} \\ &= -R^{-1}D'P_0x_n \\ &= -R^{-1}D'P_0[\Phi x_{n-1} + Du_{n-1}] \end{aligned} \tag{5.6}$$

Therefore,

$$[I + R^{-1}D'P_0D]u_{n-1} = -R^{-1}D'P_0\Phi x_{n-1}$$

Hence,

$$u_{n-1} = -[R + D'P_0D]^{-1}D'P_0\Phi x_{n-1} \tag{5.7}$$

Now, we can work backward from here

$$u_{n-2} = R^{-1}D'\lambda_{n-2} \tag{5.8}$$

$$\begin{aligned} \lambda_{n-2} &= -H'QHx_{n-1} + \Phi'\lambda_{n-1} \\ &= -H'QHx_{n-1} - \Phi'P_0x_n \\ &= -H'QHx_{n-1} - \Phi'P_0[\Phi x_{n-1} + Du_{n-1}] \\ &= -H'QHx_{n-1} - \Phi'P_0\Phi x_{n-1} + \Phi'P_0D[R + D'P_0D]^{-1} \\ &\quad \times D'P_0\Phi x_{n-1} \\ &= -H'QHx_{n-1} - \Phi'\{P_0 - P_0D[D'P_0D + R]^{-1}D'P_0\}\Phi x_{n-1} \\ &\triangleq -[H'QH + \Phi'M_1\Phi]x_{n-1} \\ &\triangleq -P_1x_{n-1} \end{aligned} \tag{5.9}$$

where

$$M_1 \triangleq P_0 - P_0D[D'P_0D + R]^{-1}D'P_0$$

$$P_1 \triangleq \Phi'M_1\Phi + H'QH$$

Now Equations 5.8 and 5.9 are in exactly the same form as Equations 5.5 and 5.6, except for the subscripts. Hence, our solution should be similar to Equation 5.7; namely,

$$u_{n-2} = -[D'P_1D + R]^{-1}D'P_1\Phi x_{n-2} \tag{5.10}$$

Continuing in this manner, we obtain the general solution by induction.

$$\begin{aligned} u_{n-i} &= -[D'P_{i-1}D + R]^{-1}D'P_{i-1}\Phi x_{n-i} \\ &\triangleq -K_{n-i}x_{n-i} \end{aligned} \tag{5.11}$$

where

$$P_i = \Phi' M_i \Phi + H'QH$$

$$M_i = P_{i-1} - P_{i-1}D(D'P_{i-1}D + R)^{-1}D'P_{i-1}$$

$$i = 1, 2, \cdots, n$$

$$P_0 \triangleq A + H'QH$$

Equation 5.11 gives a complete set of relations which specify the feedback control law for the system. Note that once P, H, Q, R, D are given, P_i, M_i, K_{n-i} can be computed readily beforehand and stored in the memory and the feedback control system requires only very simple real time computations. The block diagram of the over-all system is given in Figure 5.1.

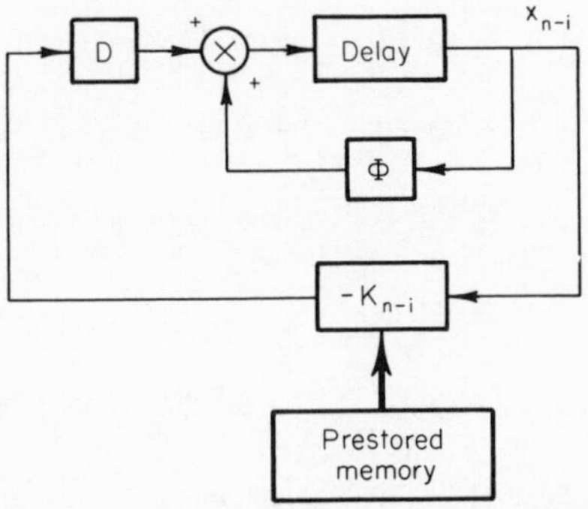

Figure 5.1. Optimal deterministic control.

Optimal control over an infinite interval: Now, let us consider the limiting case where $n \to \infty$. Equation 5.11 holds for all $i = 1, 2, \cdots, \infty$. For very large i, the matrices P_i, M_i converge toward constants P, M, which satisfy the following relations:

$$\left.\begin{aligned} P &= \Phi' M \Phi + H'QH \\ M &= P - PD(D'PD + R)^{-1}D'P \end{aligned}\right\} \tag{5.12}$$

Therefore,

$$P = \Phi' P\Phi - \Phi' PD(D' PD + R)^{-1} D' P\Phi + H' QH \quad (5.13)$$

This is a nonlinear algebraic equation; once Φ, D, R, Q, H, are given, P could be found by various iterative computation processes. Once P is determined, K could be calculated. Note that for the interval of interest, K is constant, hence the feedback control law is simply

$$u_k = - Kx_k \quad (5.14)$$

The result shown in Equation 5.14 states that the optimal feedback control law for a linear invariant system with quadratic criterion and with infinite interval is linear and invariant. This result is actually not too surprising, since similar results have been obtained by Newton, Gould, and Kaiser[44] and various others using frequency domain techniques.

5.2 Optimal Estimation and Control (Optimal Stochastic-Control Problem)

In Chapters 2 and 3, and in the earlier section of this chapter, we discussed the various methods of obtaining solutions for optimal deterministic control as well as that of estimation in a stochastic environment. In this section, we discuss the problem of control in a stochastic environment whose solution must depend on some proper cross-fertilization of these two fields of knowledge. In a stochastic environment, we do not have the precise knowledge of the states; consequently, the performance criterion must be some probability measures of the states and the purpose of control will be to influence these probability measures that are in themselves deterministic. We'll present first the so-called separation theorem.

5.2.1 Separation Theorem for Linear Systems with Quadratic Criterion and Gaussian Inputs.[9, 16, 20, 31, 54] Statement of the separation theorem: "In linear systems with quadratic error criterion and subjected to Gaussian inputs, the optimal stochastic controller is synthesized by cascading an optimal estimator with a deterministic optimal control."[9] This result is obtained by solving the optimization problem of minimizing

$$J = E\left\{ ||x_n||_A^2 + \sum_{i=1}^{N} \frac{1}{2}\left[||x_i||_Q^2 + ||u_{i-1}||_R^2 \right]\right\} \quad (5.15)$$

Given $z_0, z_1, \cdots, z_{n-1}$, and A, Q, R; subjected to the constraints

$$\left.\begin{aligned} x_{i+1} &= \Phi x_i + Du_i + \Gamma w_i \\ z_i &= Hx_i + v_i \end{aligned}\right\} \qquad (5.16)$$

where w_i and v_i are white Gaussian random sequences with zero mean and covariances Q and R, respectively. The solution is obtained via dynamic programming. Since the derivation is rather involved, we will present only the results here. (The interested reader may consult References 9 and 20 for details.) The solution is

$$\begin{aligned} u_{n-i} &= -(D'P_{i-1}D + R)^{-1}D'P_{i-1}\Phi x_{n-i|n-i} \\ &\triangleq -K_{n-i}x_{n-i|n-i} \\ P_i &= \Phi' M_i \Phi + Q \qquad P_0 \triangleq A + Q \\ M_i &= P_{i-1} - P_{i-1}D(D'P_{i-1}D + R)^{-1}D'P_{i-1} \qquad i = 1, 2, \cdots, n \end{aligned} \qquad (5.17)$$

The closed-loop controller is shown in Figure 5.2.

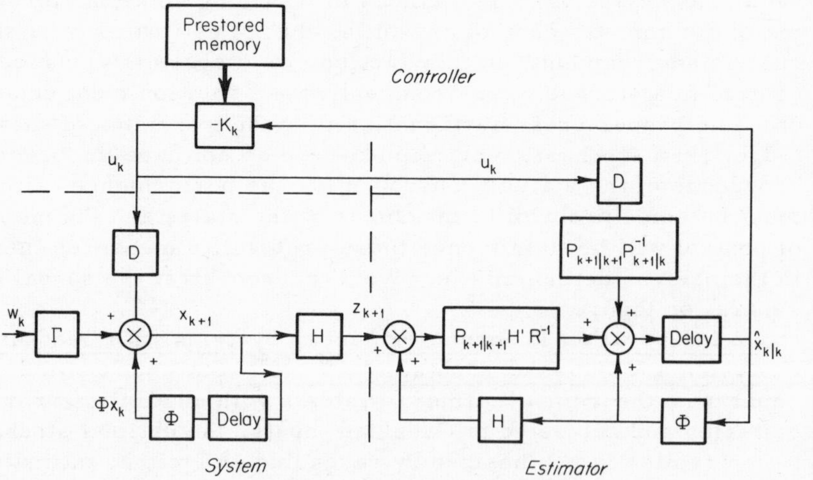

Figure 5.2. Closed-loop stochastic controller.

In all the forementioned references, one common oversight occurred in the introduction of the control input into the optimal estimator. In all cases, the covariance matrix correction term $P_{k+1|k+1}P_{k+1|k}^{-1}$ was neglected. This term must be included if we are to maintain optimality. We shall show how this term comes about via the Bayesian approach. From Equation 3.79, we have

$$p(x_k | Z_k) = \frac{p(z_k | x_k, Z_{k-1})}{p(z_k | Z_{k-1})} p(x_k | Z_{k-1}) \tag{5.18}$$

The constraint equations are

$$\left.\begin{aligned} x_k &= \Phi x_{k-1} + \Gamma w_{k-1} + Du_{k-1} \\ z_k &= Hx_k + v_k \end{aligned}\right\} \tag{5.19}$$

where w_{k-1} and v_k are independent Gaussian white random sequences, with zero mean and covariant matrix Q and R, respectively. Calculating all the component density functions and combining them, we obtain readily the following relations

$$\begin{aligned} \hat{x}_{k|k} &= \Phi\hat{x}_{k-1|k-1} + P_{k|k}H'R^{-1}[z_k - H\Phi\hat{x}_{k-1|k-1}] \\ &\quad + \underline{\underline{P_{k|k}P_{k|k-1}^{-1}}}Du_{k-1} \qquad (5.20)\dagger \\ P_{k|k} &= P_{k|k-1} - P_{k|k-1}H'(HP_{k|k-1}H' + R)^{-1}H'P_{k|k-1} \end{aligned}$$

We can give a physical interpretation to this term. Since at time k-1 if we add the term Du_{k-1} to $\Phi\hat{x}_{k-1|k-1}$, we obtain the optimal prediction $\hat{x}_{k|k-1}$. Now after the k-th measurement, the optimal estimate of x_k is $\hat{x}_{k|k}$. Since the prediction $\hat{x}_{k|k-1}$ and the estimate $\hat{x}_{k|k}$ are in general different, the control input should be modified. In this chase, the modification is the ratio of their respective covariance $P_{k|k}P_{k|k-1}^{-1}$.

5.2.2 A Simplified Control Philosophy for Optimal Closed-Loop Regulators. In this section, we generate a simplified philosophy of control. We assume that the basic physical process is such that the current (present) control can only influence future behavior of the plant. Therefore at any time, the control law must be devised such that it will make the future output more "to our liking." Consequently, we build an optimal filter and predictor, and we design our control law such that it minimizes some criterion function of the predicted outputs. To be more specific, we define the problem as follows:

Given:

1. Physical plant

$$x_{k+1} = f(x_k, u_k, w_k) \qquad z_k = g(x_k, v_k) \tag{5.21}$$

†Note: In Equation 5.20 $P_{k|k}$ stands for the covariance matrix whereas the P_i in Equation 5.17 stands for the weighting matrix for the optimal controller.

2. Optimal filter: We assume that the optimal filtering solution $\hat{x}_{k|k}$ is given at all times.
3. Optimal prediction: We assume that the optimal prediction $\hat{x}_{k+1|k}$ could be obtained from the filter output $\hat{x}_{k|k}$ and with the noise and physical characteristics, such that

$$\hat{x}_{k+1|k} = f^*(\hat{x}_{k|k}, u_k) \tag{5.22}$$

4. We will design our control law as a step-by-step single-stage† optimization process which

$$\min_{u_k} J = ||\hat{x}_{k+1|k}||^2_{Q_k^*} + ||u_k||^2_{R_k^*} \tag{5.23}$$

subject to the constraints

$$\hat{x}_{k+1|k} = f_k^*(\hat{x}_{k|k}, u_k)$$

Solving the problem, we have

$$Q_k^*[\hat{x}_{k+1|k}] + \lambda = 0$$

$$R_k^* u_k - \frac{\partial f_k^{*'}}{\partial u_k} \lambda = 0$$

Therefore,

$$u_k = - R_k^{*^{-1}} \frac{\partial f_k^*}{\partial u_k} Q_k^*[\hat{x}_{k+1|k}]$$

$$= - R_k^{*^{-1}} \frac{\partial f_k^*}{\partial u_k} Q_k^*[f_k^*(\hat{x}_{k|k}, u_k)] \tag{5.24}$$

From this simple computation, we obtain the optimal single-stage closed-loop control law (in the sense defined earlier). Once R_k^*, Q_k^*, f_k^* are given, we can solve for u_k as a function of $\hat{x}_{k|k}$ or $\hat{x}_{k+1|k}$ whichever is more convenient. It should be emphasized here that this control law is obtained using a single stage process. It is obviously nonoptimal with respect to a mul[tistage] process. The only merit lies in its simplicity. In a clos[ed-]loop optimal regulator, where the error is never very large, w[e] may expect this type of control law to exhibit behavior closely

---

†A single-stage process is assumed here to avoid the difficulties involved in solving two-point boundary-value problems, hence making the problem amenable to real time solutions.

approximating that of a multistage process if we properly choose the weighting functions Q_k^* and R_k^* such that they are time varying or proportional to the magnitude of the error (this is a conjecture). Indeed, in the case of a linear system subjected to Gaussian noise, we have

$$J = \|\hat{x}_{k+1|k}\|^2_{Q_k^*} + \|u_k\|^2_{R_k^*} \tag{5.25}$$

Putting in the constraints

$$\hat{x}_{k+1|k} = \Phi\hat{x}_{k|k} + Du_k \tag{5.26}$$

and solving, we have

$$u_k = -[R_k^* + D'Q_k^*D]^{-1}D'Q_k^*\Phi\hat{x}_{k|k} \tag{5.27}$$

This control law is identical to that of Equation 5.17 if we choose $Q_k^* \equiv P_{n-k-1}$.

5.3 Identification and Control

In this section, we consider a single-input, single-output system subjected to noise disturbance.

$$\left.\begin{aligned} x_{k+1} &= \Phi^* x_k + \Gamma w_k + du_k \\ z_k &= h^{*\prime} x_k \end{aligned}\right\} \tag{5.28}$$

where Φ^*, h^* are a canonical pair (see Chapter 4) and where the output z_k and input u_k could be measured, the Φ^*, d are unknown, and w_k is white Gaussian noise. In Chapter 4, we showed that this system could be readily transformed into an equivalent difference equation (Equation 4.63)

$$z_t = \mathscr{S}^{*\prime}_{t-1}\Phi^* + n'_{t-1}b \tag{5.29}$$

where

$$\mathscr{S}^*_{t-1} \triangleq \begin{bmatrix} z_{t-n} \\ \vdots \\ z_{t-2} \\ z_{t-1} \\ \hline u_{t-n} \\ \vdots \\ u_{t-1} \end{bmatrix} \qquad \Phi^* = \begin{bmatrix} -a_n \\ \vdots \\ -a_1 \\ \hline c_n \\ \vdots \\ c_1 \end{bmatrix} \qquad n_{t-1} = \begin{bmatrix} w_{t-n} \\ \vdots \\ w_{t-1} \end{bmatrix} \qquad b = \begin{bmatrix} b_n \\ \vdots \\ b_1 \end{bmatrix}$$

Using the method of least-squares fit, we showed that the solution of the optimal identifier is given in Equations 4.64 and 4.65. Since the noise is white and with zero mean, the best prediction is

$$\hat{z}_{n+1} = \mathcal{S}_n^{*'} \hat{\Phi}^*(n)$$

$$= \sum_{i=1}^{n} [-\hat{a}_i(n) z_{n-i+1} + \hat{c}_i(n) u_{n-i+1}] \tag{5.30}$$

where

$$\hat{\Phi}^*(n) = \begin{bmatrix} -\hat{a}_n(n) \\ \vdots \\ -\hat{a}_1(n) \\ \hline \hat{c}_n(n) \\ \vdots \\ \hat{c}_1(n) \end{bmatrix}$$

Using the same control philosophy as that of Section 5.2.2, we have

$$J \triangleq Q\hat{z}^2_{n+1|n} + Ru_n^2$$

with the constraints

$$\hat{z}_{n+1} = \mathcal{S}_n^{*'} \hat{\phi}(n) \triangleq \mathcal{S}_n^{***'} \hat{\phi}^{***}(n) + \hat{c}_1(n) u_n$$

where

$$\mathcal{S}_n^{***} \triangleq \begin{bmatrix} z_1 \\ \vdots \\ z_n \\ \hline u_1 \\ \vdots \\ u_{n-1} \end{bmatrix} \qquad \phi^{***} \triangleq \begin{bmatrix} -\hat{a}_n \\ \vdots \\ -\hat{a}_1 \\ \hline \hat{c}_n \\ \vdots \\ \hat{c}_2 \end{bmatrix}$$

Solving, we have

$$\left.\begin{aligned} Q\hat{z}_{n+1} + \lambda &= 0 \\ Ru_n - \hat{c}_1(n)\lambda &= 0 \end{aligned}\right\} \tag{5.31}$$

Therefore,

$$u_n = -\frac{\hat{c}_1(n)}{R} Q\hat{z}_{n+1|n}$$

$$= -\frac{\hat{c}_1(n)}{R} Q[\mathcal{S}_n^{***'}\hat{\phi}^{***}_{(n)} + \hat{c}_1(n)u_n]$$

Rearranging, we have

$$u_n = -\frac{\hat{c}_1(n)\,Q[\mathcal{S}_n^{***'}\hat{\phi}^{***}_{(n)}]}{[R + \hat{c}_1(n)^2 Q]} \qquad (5.32)$$

Hence the block diagram of this regulator is as shown in Figure 5.3.

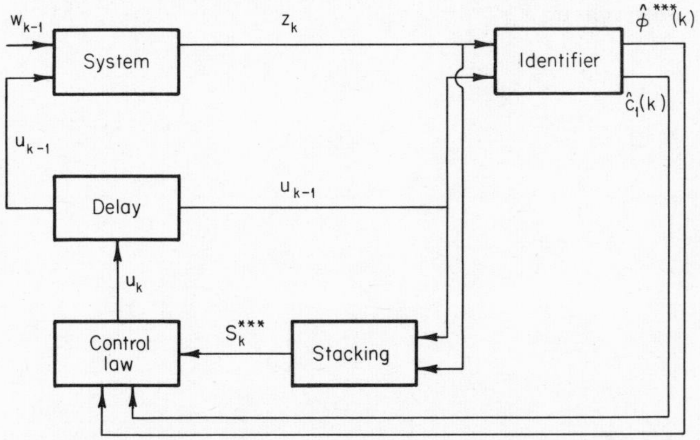

Figure 5.3. Adaptive regulator block diagram.

It should be emphasized here that this configuration is but a conjecture. It is a reasonable thing to do, whether it has any merits remains to be investigated.

5.4 Summary

In this chapter, we discussed the problem of obtaining closed-loop optimal-control laws. It was shown that in the deterministic case, closed-loop control law could be readily obtained for linear systems with quadratic criteria. The result of the separation theorem was also presented. This theorem states that for a linear system with quadratic criterion subjected to Gaussian input, the closed-loop control system is made by cascading an optimal estimator and an optimal deterministic controller. A simplified closed-loop control philosophy was also developed. This philosophy begins by separating the controller from the estimator and predictor. The basic idea here is that of using the control input to minimize the prediction error. One advantage of this type of approach is that we are always solving a deterministic control problem, once the optimal estimator and prediction are obtained. Of course, in many cases we desire the solution of a multistage control process instead of the single-stage process shown; however, in such cases we must solve a two-point boundary-value problem, and the solution becomes much more complicated. It is conjectured that in a closed-loop regulator-type process where the errors are usually small, the cascading of optimal single-stage processes may be made to approximate optimal multistage processes if we choose the criterion with some logic (that is, magnitude of the error, and so forth). Using this simplified philosophy, an optimal closed-loop identification and control process is concocted. Its stability and performance remains to be investigated.

Chapter 6

RECOMMENDATIONS FOR FUTURE INVESTIGATION

There is an old saying that when one reaches the peak of a mountain, one only finds more and higher mountains. Indeed, at the conclusion of this study, we found that there are numerous interesting and unsolved problems. Several of these are discussed in this chapter.

1. Optimal estimators for linear systems subjected to non-Gaussian noise: We could begin by using the conjugate distributions discussed in Reference 49 and the Bayesian approach.

2. Weighted least-squares method: The technique developed in Chapter 4 tends to tolerate larger percentage errors in parameters of smaller magnitude than in larger ones. This is true because we have weighted all the error magnitudes equally. It would be desirable to develop a scheme that weights all the percentage errors equally.

3. Optimum adaptive system: One of the interesting problems arising in the couse of this study is, "In a linear system with quadratic criterion, is the system, shown in Figure 6.1, obtained by cascading an optimal estimator, identifier, and controller optimal over all?"

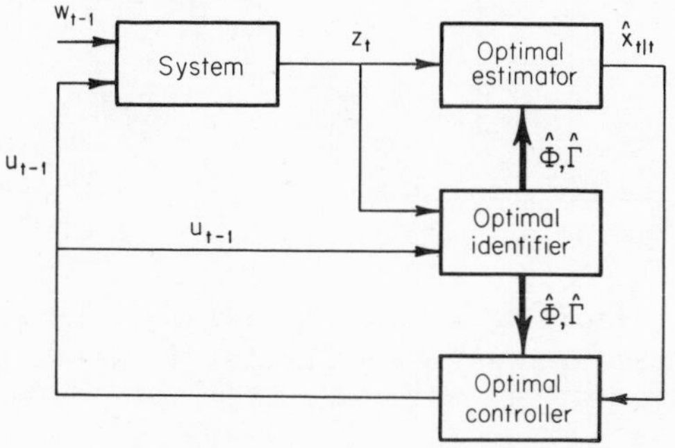

Figure 6.1. Block diagram of optimal adaptive controller.

This is an interesting, but difficult problem, since the over-all system is nonlinear.

4. Guidance and control integration: Note that the basic computational schemes developed for identification, estimation, and even that of control of linear systems are very similar. In Reference 3, it was shown that the optimal estimation scheme could

be used to obtain trajectory parameters. Hence the part of identification, estimation, and control of both the guidance and control of a space vehicle could be solved by a single computational program. This is ideally suited to applications in which we wish to time-share a centralized on-board digital computer since only peripheral equipment needs to be changed. This may be a fruitful area for further research.

5. Stochastic approximations: This is an area of research with the objective of developing a simplified but consistent identification (estimation) scheme. References 14 and 51 suggested various regressive schemes that converge to the desired value with probability one. In References 17 and 24 Ho applied this idea to the identification of a linear system with unknown characteristics. It is assumed that all states are measureable. The resultant scheme is

$$\hat{\phi}^i_{t+1} = \hat{\phi}^i_t + \rho_t[x^i_{t+1} - \hat{\phi}^i_t x_t] x_t$$

where

$$x_{t+1} = \Phi x_t + \Gamma w_t \qquad w_t \text{ white Gaussian noise}$$

$$\Phi \triangleq \begin{bmatrix} \phi^1 \\ \phi^2 \\ \vdots \\ \phi^n \end{bmatrix} \qquad \phi^i \triangleq \text{i-th row of } \Phi \qquad \rho_t \triangleq \frac{1}{\lambda t} \qquad \lambda = \text{const}$$

and where x^i is the i-th component of the state vector. The detailed convergence properties of this scheme have not been investigated.

In the case where we cannot measure all the state variables, such as the case discussed in Chapter 4, we suggest the following scheme:

$$\hat{\phi}_{t+1} = \hat{\phi}_t + \rho_t \mathscr{S}_t [z_{t+1} - \mathscr{S}'_t \hat{\phi}_t]$$

where

$$\rho(t) = \frac{1}{\lambda + t} \qquad \lambda = \text{const}$$

(All the symbols used here are consistent with that of Chapter 4.) This scheme can be called the method of the local gradient, since the correction term is the local gradient obtained by

$$\frac{\partial}{\partial \phi_t} J = \frac{\partial}{\partial \phi_t} ||z_{t+1} - \mathcal{S}_t' \hat{\phi}_t||^2$$

The constant λ is chosen from Reference 14 to assure convergence. The author has put this scheme on the computer, but so far the results have not been conclusive.

Appendix A

VECTOR DIFFERENTIATION

1. The derivative of a vector with respect to a scalar is a (column) vector;

$$\frac{db}{dx_1} \triangleq \begin{bmatrix} \frac{db_1}{dx_1} \\ \frac{db_2}{dx_1} \\ \vdots \\ \frac{db_n}{dx_1} \end{bmatrix} \qquad x_1 = \text{scalar}$$

2. The derivative of a scalar with respect to a vector is a row vector;

$$\frac{db_1}{dx} \triangleq \left[\frac{db_1}{dx_1}, \frac{db_1}{dx_2}, \ldots, \frac{db_1}{dx_n} \right] \qquad b_1 = \text{scalar}$$

3. The differential of a vector with respect to a vector is a matrix;

$$\frac{db}{dx} = \begin{bmatrix} \frac{db_1}{dx_1}, & \frac{db_1}{dx_2}, & \ldots, & \frac{db_1}{dx_n} \\ \vdots & & & \vdots \\ \frac{db_n}{dx_1} & & \ldots & \frac{db_n}{dx_n} \end{bmatrix} = \begin{bmatrix} \frac{db_1}{dx} \\ \frac{db_2}{dx} \\ \vdots \\ \frac{db_n}{dx} \end{bmatrix}$$

where b, x are n × 1 vectors.

4. The second derivative of a scalar with respect to a vector is a matrix;

$$\frac{d^2 b_1}{dx^2} \triangleq \frac{d}{dx} \quad \frac{db_1}{dx}' = \frac{d}{dx} \begin{bmatrix} \frac{db_1}{dx_1} \\ \vdots \\ \frac{db_1}{dx_n} \end{bmatrix}$$

$$\triangleq \begin{bmatrix} \frac{d^2 b_1}{dx_1^2}, & \frac{d^2 b_1}{dx_1\, dx_2}, & \ldots, & \frac{d^2 b_1}{dx_1\, dx_n} \\ \frac{d^2 b_1}{dx_2\, dx_1} & \frac{d^2 b_1}{dx_2^2}, & \ldots, & \frac{d^2 b_1}{dx_2\, dx_n} \\ \vdots & & & \vdots \\ \frac{d^2 b_1}{dx_n\, dx_1} & & \ldots & \frac{d^2 b_1}{dx_n^2} \end{bmatrix}$$

5. Differentiation of a scalar product with respect to a vector is a row vector;

$$\frac{d\langle a, b\rangle}{dx} \triangleq \frac{d}{dx}(a'b)$$

$$\triangleq a' \frac{db}{dx} + b' \frac{da}{dx}$$

6. Differentiation of a quadratic form is a row vector;

$$\frac{d}{dx}[x'Ax] = \frac{d}{dx}\langle x, Ax\rangle = x'AI + x'A'I$$

$$= 2x'A$$

since A is symmetric.

7. Differentiation of a linear form with respect to x is a constant row vector;

$$\frac{d}{dx}[\lambda' Ax] \triangleq \lambda' A \qquad \lambda = \text{const vector}$$

8. Time derivatives are

$$\frac{d}{dt}\langle x, y\rangle = \langle \frac{dx}{dt}, y\rangle + \langle x, \frac{dy}{dt}\rangle$$

$$\frac{d}{dt} Ax = \frac{dA}{dt} x + A \frac{dx}{dt}$$

$$\frac{d}{dt} AB = A \frac{dB}{dt} + \frac{dA}{dt} B$$

$$\frac{d}{dt} [A^{-1}] = - A^{-1} \frac{dA}{dt} A^{-1}$$

$$\frac{d}{dt} (A^n) = \frac{dA}{dt} A^{n-1} + A \frac{dA}{dt} A^{n-2} + \cdots + A^{n-1} \frac{dA}{dt}$$

Appendix B

BASIC COMPUTATION PROGRAM EQUATIONS

B.1 Basic Equations for Computational Program 1

$$\phi_{t+1} = \Psi^{(1)} \phi_t + \alpha_t \qquad \phi_0 \text{ given} \tag{B.1}$$

α_t is white Gaussian with mean $\overline{\alpha}$ and covariance matrix Q^*.

$$x_{t+1} = \Phi_t x_t + \Gamma w_t \qquad x_0 \text{ given} \tag{B.2}$$

w_t is white Gaussian noise with mean $\overline{w}$ and covariance matrix Q.

$$\Phi_t = \left[\begin{array}{c|c} \begin{matrix} 0 \\ 0 \\ 0 \\ 0 \end{matrix} & I \\ \hline \multicolumn{2}{c}{\phi_t'} \end{array}\right] \qquad \Phi_0 \text{ given} \tag{B.3}$$

$$z_t = h' x_t + v_t \tag{B.4}$$

v_t is white Gaussian noise with mean $\overline{v}$ and covariance matrix R.

$$M_{t+1} = \Psi P_t \Psi' + B \qquad P_0 \text{ given, } B = \text{const } \dagger \tag{B.5}$$

$$K_{t+1} = M_{t+1} \mathcal{S}_t (\mathcal{S}_t' M_{t+1} \mathcal{S}_t + 1)^{-1} \tag{B.6}$$

$$P_{t+1} = M_{t+1} - K_{t+1} \mathcal{S}_t' M_{t+1} \tag{B.7}$$

$$\hat{\phi}_{t+1} = \Psi \hat{\phi}_t + K_{t+1} \left(z_{t+1} - \mathcal{S}_t' \Psi \hat{\phi}_t \right) \qquad \hat{\phi}_0 \text{ given} \tag{B.8}$$

†Note: B is a constant matrix chosen by experimentation. It should be proportional to Q^*.

$$\mathscr{S}_t = \begin{bmatrix} z_{t-n+1} \\ \vdots \\ z_{t-1} \\ z_t \end{bmatrix} \qquad \mathscr{S}_0 \text{ given} \tag{B.9}$$

B.2 Basic Equations for Computational Program 2

$$\phi_{t+1} = \Psi \phi_t + \alpha_t \qquad \phi_0,\ Q^*, \overline{\alpha} \text{ given} \tag{B.10}$$

$$\left.\begin{aligned} z_t &= -a_1 z_{t-1} - a_2 z_{t-2} - \cdots - a_n z_{t-n} \\ &\quad + b_1 u_{t-1} + b_2 u_{t-2} + \cdots + b_n u_{t-n} + w_{t-1} \\ &= \mathscr{S}_{t-1}^{*\prime} \phi^* + w_{t-1} \\ u_t &= \text{some chosen control law} \end{aligned}\right\} \tag{B.11}$$

$$M_{t+1} = \Psi P_t \Psi' + B \qquad P_0 \text{ given, } B = \text{const} \tag{B.12}$$

$$K_{t+1} = M_{t+1} \mathscr{S}_t^* (\mathscr{S}_t^{*\prime} M_{t+1} \mathscr{S}_t^* + 1)^{-1} \tag{B.13}$$

$$P_{t+1} = M_{t+1} - K_{t+1} \mathscr{S}_t^{*\prime} M_{t+1} \tag{B.14}$$

$$\hat{\phi}_{t+1}^* = \Psi \hat{\phi}_t^* + K_{t+1} \left(z_{t+1} - \mathscr{S}_t^{*\prime} \Psi \hat{\phi}_t^* \right) \qquad \hat{\phi}_0^* \text{ given} \tag{B.15}$$

$$\mathscr{S}_{t-1}^* = \begin{bmatrix} z_{t-n} \\ \vdots \\ z_{t-2} \\ z_{t-1} \\ \hline u_{t-n} \\ \vdots \\ u_{t-2} \\ u_{t-1} \end{bmatrix} \qquad \phi^* = \begin{bmatrix} -a_n \\ \vdots \\ -a_2 \\ -a_1 \\ \hline b_n \\ \vdots \\ b_1 \end{bmatrix} \tag{B.16}$$

REFERENCES

1. Andeen, R. E., and P. P. Shipley, "Digital Adaptive Flight Control System," ASD-TDR-62-61; or ASTIA AD 282880 (May, 1962).

2. Athans, M., "Optimal Control Theory," Lecture Notes, M.I.T., (1962).

3. Battin, R., "Optimizing a Statistical Navigation Procedure for Space Flight," Am. Rocket Soc., 32, 1681-1696 (November, 1962).

4. Bellman, R., Adaptive Control — A Guided Tour, Princeton University Press, Princeton, N.J. (1960).

5. Bellman, R., and S. Dreyfus, Applied Dynamic Programming, Princeton University Press, Princeton, N.J. (1962).

6. Bryson, A. E., F. J. Caroll, K. Mikami, W. Denham, "Determination of the Lift or Drag Programs that Minimizes Re-Entry Heating," J. Aerospace Sci., 29, No. 4 (April, 1962)

7. Bryson, A. E., and W. Denham, "A Steepest Descent Method for Solving Optimum Programming Problems," ASME Conf. Mech., Chicago, Ill. (June, 1961).

8. Bryson, A. E., and M. Frazier, "Smoothing in Linear and Nonlinear Systems," Proc. Optimal System Synthesis Symposium, Wright Field, Ohio, ASD-TDR-63-119 (September, 1962).

9. Bryson, A. E., and Y. C. Ho, Lecture Notes, "Optimization of Dynamic Systems," Harvard University Summer Course (July, 1963).

10. Breakwell, J. V., and A. E. Bryson, "Neighboring Optimum Terminal Control for Multivariable Nonlinear Systems," J. Soc. Ind. Appl, Mech., Control, I, No. 2 (1963).

11. Chang, S. S. L., "A Modified Maximum Principle for Optimal Control of Systems with Bounded Phase Space Coordinates," JACC Preprint, pp. 1-3 (1963).

12. Davenport, Jr., W. B., and W. L. Root, Random Signal and Noise, McGraw-Hill Book Co., Inc., New York (1958).

13. Dreyfus, S., "Numerical Solution of Variational Problems," Rand Report, P-2374 (1962).

14. Dvoretzky, A., "On Stochastic Approximation," Third Berkeley Symposium Prob. and Math. Stat., University of California (1954).

15. Gregory, P. C., "Proceedings of the Self Adaptive Flight Control Symposium," WADC TR 54-49; ASTIA AD 209389 (March, 1959).

16. Gunckel, T. L., "Optimal Design of Sampled Data System with Random Parameters," Stanford University Electronics Lab., Report 2102-2 (April 24, 1961).

17. Ho, Y.C., "A Method for the Identification of Stationary Linear Systems and Random Sequences," Sperry-Rand, Report SRRC-RR-63-10 (1963).

18. Ho, Y. C., "A Successive Approximation Technique for Optimum Control System Subjected to Input Saturation," JACC Preprint (June, 1961).

19. Ho, Y. C., "Computational Procedure for Optimal Control Problems with State Variable Constraints," Rand Report, P-2402 (1962).

20. Ho, Y. C., Lecture Notes, "Advanced Control Methods," Harvard University (1962).

21. Ho, Y. C., "On Stochastic Approximation and Optimal Filtering Methods," J. Math. Anal. Appl., 6, No. 1 (February, 1963).

22. Ho, Y. C., and P. B. Brentani, "On Computing Optimal Control with Inequality Constraints," Symposium Multivariable Control System, Soc. Ind. Appl. Math., Fall Meeting, Cambridge, Mass. (1962).

23. Ho, Y. C., and R. C. K. Lee, "A Bayesian Approach to Problems in Stochastic Estimation and Control," JACC Preprint, XIV-2 (1964).

24. Ho, Y. C., and B. Whalen, "An Approach to the Identification and Control of Linear Dynamic System with Unknown Coefficients," Trans. AIEE, AC-8, No. 3, 255-256 (July, 1963).

25. Jaynes, E. T., "Probability Theory in Science and Engineering," Colloquium Lectures in Pure and Applied Science, No. 4, Stanford University (1958); published by Field Research Lab., Socony Mobil Oil Co., Inc., Dallas, Texas

26. Kalman, R. E., "A New Approach to Linear Filtering and Prediction Problems," Trans. ASME, J. Basic Engineering (March, 1960).

27. Kalman, R. E., "Design of a Self Optimizing Control System," Trans. ASME (February, 1958).

28. Kalman, R. E., "The Theory of Optimal Control and the Calculus of Variation," RIAS, Report 61-3 (1961).

29. Kalman, R. E., "The Variational Principle of Adaptation Filters for Curve Fitting," Intern. Federation in Automatic Control, Rome (1962).

30. Kalman, R. E. and R. S. Bucy, "New Results in Linear Filtering and Prediction Theory," Trans. ASME, J. Basic Engineering (1961).

31. Kalman, R. E., T. S. Englar, and R. S. Bucy, "Fundamental Study of Adaptive Control Systems," ASD-TR-61-27, I (April, 1962).

32. Kelley, H. J., "Gradient Theory of Optimal Flight Paths," J. Am. Rocket Soc., 30 (October, 1960).

33. Kelley, H. J., R. E. Kopp, and H. G. Moyer, "Successive Approximation Techniques for Trajectory Optimization," Proc. Inst. Aero. Sci. Symposium Vehicle System Optimization, Garden City, N.Y. (November, 1961).

34. Kopp, R. E. and R. J. Orford, "Linear Regression to System Identification for Adaptive Systems," J. AIAA, 1, No. 10, 2300-2306 (November, 1962).

35. Laning, J. H., Jr., and R. H. Battin, Random Process in Automatic Control, McGraw-Hill Book Co., Inc., New York (1956).

36. Lee, R. C. K., and V. Folkner, "Adaptive Control System for Large Elastic Boosters," IRE Adaptive Control Symposium, Garden City, L.I. (September, 1960).

37. Lee, R. C. K., and J. F. L. Lee, "Analysis and Design of a Digital Adaptive Flight Control System," SAE Committee A-18 Meeting on Digital Systems, Washington, D.C. (June, 1961).

38. Lee, Y. W., Statistical Theory of Communication, John Wiley & Sons, Inc., New York (1960).

39. Leitmann, G., Optimization Techniques, Academic Press Inc., New York (1962).

40. Lendaris, G., "The Identification of Linear Sampled Data Systems," Trans. AIEE, Part III (September, 1962).

41. Li, Y.T., and H. P. Whitaker, "Performance Characterization for Adaptive Control Systems," Intern. Federation in Automatic Control (IFAC), Rome (April, 1962).

42. Mellen, D. L., "Application of Adaptive Flight Control," Intern. Federation in Automatic Control, (IFAC), Rome (April, 1962).

43. Mishkin, E., and L. Braun, Adaptive Control Systems, McGraw-Hill Brook Co., Inc., New York (1961).

44. Newton, G. C., L. A. Gould, and J. F. Kaiser, Analytical Design of Linear Feedback Systems, John Wiley & Sons, Inc., New York (1957).

45. Osburn, P. V., "Investigation of a Method of Adaptive Control," Sc. D. Thesis, M.I.T., Dept. of Aeronautics and Astronautics (1961).

46. Penrose, R., "On the Generalized Inverse of a Matrix," Proc. Cambridge Phil. Soc., 51, pp. 406-413 (1955).

47. Penrose, R., "The Best Approximation to the Solution of Matrix Equations," Proc. Cambridge Phil. Soc., 52, pp. 17-19 (1956).

48. Pontryagin, L. S., V. G. Boltyanski, R. V. Gamkrelidge, and E. F. Mishchenko, The Mathematical Theory of Optimal Processes, Interscience Publishers, Inc., New York (1962).

49. Raiffa, H., and R. Schlaifer, Applied Statistical Decision Theory, Harvard University Press, Cambridge, Mass. (1961).

50. Rauch, H., F. Tung, and C. Striebel, "On the Maximum Likelihood Estimate for Linear Systems," Lockheed Missile and Space Co., Technical Report (June 5, 1963).

51. Robbins, H., and S. Monro, "A Stochastic Approximation Method," Annals of Math. Stat., 22, pp. 400-407 (1951).

52. Rozonoer, L. I., "L. S. Pontryagin's Maximum Principle in Optimal Control Theory," Automation and Remote Control, 1, 20, I, II, III (October, November, December, 1959).

53. Tompkins, C. B., "Method of Steepest Descent," Modern Mathematics for the Engineer, Chap. 18, McGraw-Hill Book Co., Inc., New York (1956).

54. Tou, J. T., and P. D. Joseph, "A Study of Digital Adaptive Control System," Part II, ASTIA AD 265268 (August, 196

55. Zontendigk, G., Methods of Feasible Directions, Elsevier Publishing Company, Netherlands (1960).

56. WADD TR 60-201 "A Study to Determine the Feasibility of a Self-Optimizing Automatic Flight Control System," Aeronutronic (June, 1960); ASTIA AD 240992.

GENERAL REFERENCES

Bellman, R., An Introduction to Matrix Analysis, McGraw-Hill Book Co., Inc., New York (1960).

Desoer, C. A., "An Introduction to State Space Techniques and Linear Systems," JACC Preprint, pp. 10-12 (June 27-29, 1962).

Hildebrand, Francis B., Methods of Applied Mathematics, Prentice-Hall, Inc., Englewood Cliffs, N.J. (1952).

LaSalle, J. P., "Time Optimal Control Systems," RIAS Monograph, 59-4.

Mood, A. M., Introduction to the Theory of Statistics, McGraw-Hill Book Co., Inc., New York (1950).

Schmidt, S., "State Space Techniques Applied to the Design of a Space Navigation System," JACC Preprint (1962).

Stone, C. R., C. W. Johnson, et.al., "Time Optimal Control," Honeywell Report, R-ED6134 (September, 1959).

Zadeh, L. A., and J. Eaton, "Optimal Pursuit Strategy for Probabilistic Discrete Systems," Trans. ASME, J. Basic Eng. (March, 1962).

Zadeh, L. A., "An Introduction to State-Space Techniques," JACC Preprint, 10-11 (June 27-29, 1962).

"Identification Problems in Communication and Control Systems," Proceedings of the Princeton University Conference (March 21-22, 1963).

INDEX